FIVE CONTEMPLATIONS BY THICH NHAT HANH

This food is the gift of the whole universe: the earth, the sky, numerous living beings and much hard, loving work.

~

May we eat with mindfulness and gratitude so as to be worthy to receive it.

~

May we recognize and transform our unwholesome mental formations, especially our greed, and learn to eat with moderation.

May we keep our compassion alive by eating in such a way that we reduce the suffering of living beings, preserve the planet, and be aware of the consequences to our environment.

~

We accept this food so we may nurture our loved ones, strengthen our community, and nourish our ideal of serving all living beings.

GUILT FREE VEGAN
COOKBOOK
OIL, SUGAR, GLUTEN AND DAIRY FREE VEGETARIAN RECIPES

NANDINI GULATI • MALA BARUA

PHOTOGRAPHS
ANSHIKA VARMA

FOOD STYLING
MALA BARUA • ANSHIKA VARMA

Lustre Press
Roli Books

Second impression

© Roli Books, 2017
© Text: Mala Barua & Nandini Gulati
© Photographs: Anshika Varma

First published by Roli Books in 2015
M-75, Greater Kailash II Market
New Delhi-110 048, India
Phone: ++91-11-4068 2000
E-mail: info@rolibooks.com
Website: www.rolibooks.com

ISBN: 978-93-5194-115-6

Editors: Neeta Dutta, Rayman Gill Rai
Design: Sneha Pamneja
Pre-press: Jyoti Dey
Production: Shaji Sahadevan

Printed and bound in India by Nutech Print Services, New Delhi

CONTENTS

FOREWORD

Dr Nandita Shah

Founder, SHARAN – Sanctuary for Health and Reconnection to Animals and Nature

I have been a practicing doctor in India since 1981. When I was a child, life in India was very different from the way it is today. We visited restaurants only when we were travelling or for a celebration. Today, eating out is commonplace and in fact, many people have no idea how to cook. What makes matters worse is our disconnect from the food that we eat. Modern day urbanites have never been to a farm or an orchard. For them, food comes from the supermarket. For many, it's difficult to differentiate between real food and the 'food products' found in grocery stores.

As a child, I was always interested in health. I avoided soft drinks as I saw them as a mixture of chemicals in water. Sugar too was not a part of my life. It was only natural for me to become a homeopath because it's a holistic form of treatment with relatively less side effects. Having been brought up in a vegetarian family, I considered milk as the ideal food and consumed considerable quantities of it in various forms.

Soon after I finished my education in medicine, I became aware of the intense cruelty associated with the consumption of dairy. Artificial insemination is just a fancy word for the exploition of an animal just so that she can produce milk for our consumption. Ethically, I felt that I had to stop consuming dairy, and so my vegan journey began.

In my quest to understand more, I read Dean Ornish's book *Reversing Heart Disease*, where I learnt that he had helped people reverse their need for bypass surgery on an almost plant-based diet! Ornish stated that his book was about healing the mind, body, and spirit, which I found very appealing.

I read more and more. I could not stop. It got me thinking that human beings were the only animals that suffered lifestyle diseases, whereas animals that live in nature never come close to being obese or get diabetes and heart disease. I read John Mcdougall and Neal Barnard and learnt that diseases, thought to be incurable, could in fact be reversed! It was not an exception; with a plant-based diet, it was the norm.

I could see that the human anatomy is like that of an herbivore, and more specifically, a frugivore. Putting the wrong fuel in our body can be likened to putting diesel in a petrol car. The ride cannot be smooth. The more I thought about it, the more I could see the flaws in our medical education, which is aimed at medicine rather than food, at sickness rather than health. Our body is always healing, given a chance. We need to correct our fuel. By now, I had started experiencing the incredible health and mental benefits of a healthy, plant-based diet. I lost weight, gained flexibility, I rarely fell sick, I looked younger, and my skin started to glow.

When I became a doctor, five per cent of the adult population in India had diabetes. Today, a little over three decades later, that figure is thirty-five per cent. What has changed is the way we eat and what we eat. We are eating animal products, and more refined and processed foods than ever before, and we are paying for this with our health.

I gradually changed my practice from treating people to teaching them to heal themselves. Humans are the only animals that systematically make their foods less nutritious by refining them. Oils, sugar, white rice, and white flour are perfect examples of refined foods that are used every day. The maximum nutrition of most foods is found just under their peels. When we peel fruits and vegetables, we are refining them too.

I started telling my patients about a plant-based diet to get well. I found that those who were extremely sick, and who were given little hope by their doctors were the ones who listened intently and followed all my advice. They were able to get off medications and back on their feet in very little time! A patient of mine in his 60's, who had had diabetes for three decades along with severe manic-depressive psychosis and deteriorating eyesight due to his high blood sugar, went on a plant-based diet on my recommendation. He not only dropped his medication, but his eyesight was recovered and his depression also disappeared.

Another patient, a 70-year-old woman suffering from heart disease for three years was discharged from the intensive cardiac unit, exhausted, and with a prescription that was a page long. She agreed to switch to a plant-based diet and was off all medications in a matter of months. I see her jogging sometimes now at the ripe age of 80 in Pondicherry.

I found that many of the diseases that are considered chronic – obesity, hypertension, heart disease, diabetes, hypothyroidism, migraine headaches, menstrual disturbances, colds, coughs, sinusitis, asthma, gastro-intestinal problems, acidity, constipation, kidney and bladder problems as well as a host of allergies and auto immune problems could be prevented or reversed by going on an organic, whole plant-based diet.

My experience has shown me that without exception, everyone will see positive changes when they switch to a plant-based diet, provided deficiencies like vitamin B12 and vitamin D are looked after. Most people will be able to get off most of their medications, if not all.

With all this in mind, I founded an organization – SHARAN (India). SHARAN stands for Sanctuary for Health and Reconnection to Animals and Nature. Today SHARAN is at the forefront of lifestyle-disease prevention and reversal in India.

The greatest tragedy of our modern existence is that few people have time to cook or want to cook. Unfortunately, we are busy learning many skills and doing many other things but we forget to learn the very skill that our life depends on – preparing and eating good healthy food. We are what we eat.

I insist on serving healthy food at most of our events. People need to experience that healthy food can be at least as delicious, if not more, than the over-processed food that they are currently eating.

It was through SHARAN events that I met Nandini Gulati and Mala Barua. Nandini lived a typical urban corporate life until she decided to improve her own health and re-educated herself as a holistic health coach. She understands the difficulties that the average person faces when dealing with the challenge of changing their diets and guides them on how to make the shift. She has regularly conducted talks, potlucks, and cooking classes in the Delhi area for SHARAN over and above her private consultations and her health blog. For the past several years, she has regularly been one of the main facilitators in our 21-day programme where she is able to guide our participants on their own path of eating consciously, and living healthfully.

Mala Barua is a Wellness Expert specializing in Yoga, Tai Chi and Inner Silence Meditation. She has travelled the world with her company, Mystic Asia, and is a wellness writer for several prominent magazines. I personally experienced her passion, creativity, and expertise in exotic yet healthy cooking through several meals in her home. This led me to invite her as an expert cooking facilitator in SHARAN's 21-day disease reversal programme. When Mala creates a dish, not only is it delicious but it's also a work of art. Both Nandini and Mala have had a lot of experience in making food delicious using whole plant-based ingredients.

While plenty of such recipes can be found on the SHARAN website, this book is for especially those epicures who enjoy cooking and serving exotic, delicious, plant-based meals. With these recipes, you can 'wow' your guests and if you don't tell them that you have not used any oil and that all the food is whole and plant based, they may never know. Surprise them! Everyone needs someone to show them that healthy eating need not be a deprivation.

It's been a great honour for me to introduce you to this book by Nandini and Mala. Enough has been said about the benefits of a plant-based diet, now it is time to start cooking delicious meals. Enjoy!

August, 2015

NANDINI'S STORY

Like any non-vegetarian Punjabi family, we were extremely fond of eating. My dear departed father loved food and was always eager to try new cuisines and dishes. If there was a new restaurant, bakery, or *mithai* shop in town, we would be among the first to try it out.

I ate whenever food was available, whether I was hungry or not. I ate for taste, for variety, for bonding, for stimulation, for entertainment, and when it was free. It was compulsive, bordering on abusive.

As I grew older, such unconscious eating took its toll on my body. I was about 30 kilos overweight and had a general sense of 'un-wellbeing'. I was diagnosed with hypertension and put on daily medications. Later, I developed rheumatoid arthritis. I also had signs of early diabetes.

Desperate, I started exploring natural healing and healthy eating through websites, books, and videos. What I learned helped me re-connect with my body and develop a holistic perspective on health, beyond the prevalent paradigm of sickness and medications.

Finally, I was able to release the excess weight. I came off all the medicines I was taking for high blood pressure and my blood sugar returned to normal.

The main practices that helped me expand my awareness were:

1) Mindful Eating – paying attention to what I was eating, where it came from and its effects on my body, other sentient beings, and the environment.
2) Body Awareness – listening to the signals of the body and acting accordingly, for example, eating only when I was hungry.
3) Self-love – loving my body exactly as it was and treating it with understanding and kindness.

One summer afternoon in 2011, during the practice of mindfulness while eating chicken, I started to think about the life of the bird that now graced my plate. A feeling arose within me that this was the last piece of meat that I would be consuming. I went vegetarian.

Six days later, a friend handed me a copy of *The China Study*, which provides scientific evidence about the adverse health effects of dairy products. I decided to quit dairy. Within a month, I felt clean from within, and after three months, I was more energetic than ever before. Thus, I went from non-veg to vegan within fifteen days, and never looked back.

A few months later, I attended Dr. Nandita Shah's seminar and learnt more about a 'whole-food, plant based' diet. When I tasted the peanut curd *raita* and banana ice cream they had made for lunch; I knew that I could do this for life!

Learning to eat consciously, for me, has been a profound journey within. Through it, I have understood the larger consequences that our lifestyle choices have on the world. I have a better grasp of food history and politics. I understand the importance of eating organic food, waste composting, and the joys of growing edible plants.

I now work to spread this awareness to others as a public speaker and health coach for individuals and organisations and through my blog and social media.

I have been co-facilitating SHARAN's 21-day disease reversal programme where I met Mala. Continuing our friendship in Delhi, she fed me many a delicious and creative meal. The idea for this book came about over one such meal together.

Now, we want to share our love for healthy, tasty food with you. So spread out your favourite tablecloth, light a candle, put on some music, lay your best tableware, and invite your friends over for a restaurant-style meal at home – only this time it is compassionate, conscious, wholesome, and nourishing.

Bon Appetit!

MALA'S JOURNEY

I grew up in Assam where a meal without fish was not considered a meal. We used to go to the open wet market and watch our parents buy live fish for lunch. On days when we had guests for dinner, a special menu with chicken was cooked. We often watched the chicken heads being chopped off in our back garden and were gleefully fascinated by the severed head moving on its own on the floor. No one was sensitive to the life of the animal. Most of us grow up in rural India with such experiences.

I came to conscious eating as a progressive evolution of my spiritual journey under the tutelage of my spiritual teacher Swami Anubhavananda. My work with Mystic-Asia constantly demanded me to be healthy in mind and body. My wellness consultancy work with beautiful spas and wellness resorts all over the world had me constantly surrounded by all things healthy and beautiful. My Yoga, Tai Chi, and Inner Silence Meditation practices all helped me to become more sensitive energetically.

Yet there was this nagging urge to go one step further. I needed to align myself with my Inner practices more fully. Vegetarianism was constantly knocking at my door. At the turn of 40, my body began to respond differently to the food I was consuming. I knew I had to change. If I had gluten my body would bloat up, if I had non-vegetarian I began feeling guilty, if I had cheese I was reminded of my increasing weight. I knew I could not continue to eat the same way I did as a teenager.

One misty morning in 2011 in Delhi, my 16-year-old dog Sequoia was in the park and I watched her collapse right into her own pee as her hind legs gave way. I felt her dignity fall away in a second. She looked embarrassed, humiliated, and helpless as we had to lift her back to her feet. That was the defining moment. It was time for her to say goodbye to the world. It was not easy to take that decision and my sons were equally torn in their conflict. As I watched her eyes in her last moments, I said to my boys (all three of us with tears rolling down our cheeks) that we are crying only because we are attached to Sequoia. What about the thousands of animals that are subjected to inhuman treatment?

Something clicked and I promised Sequioa then, that I would discourage eating any more animals. It increased my awareness, consciousness, and compassion. In this confused maze of trying to find the right direction, I met Dr Nandita Shah who invited me to her 21-day disease reversal progamme to conduct some Inner Silence meditations. I was introduced to a plant-based, oil-free, sugar free, vegan diet. After 21 days of eating this, I felt a huge weight lift off me. I felt totally FREE of all my confusions over my choice of food. THIS WAS IT. There was no more confusion as to how I should eat. And nothing but organic would be good enough. I felt an immense sense of freedom. The combination was just right. I started experimenting with new ideas and began making my own recipes. The next year, Dr Nandita invited me to be the food consultant for the programme and as more ideas poured in, this book began to take shape! Nandini was instrumental in convincing me to co-write this book with her. Everytime I cooked for her at home, it was plastered on Facebook within minutes! She is my greatest inspiration!

So we came to name the book *Guilt Free* because of the freedom it offers us in so many areas and personally, I dedicate this book to my beloved Sequoia.

The following prayer of Metta, seems appropriate to offer along with the book:

May you be filled with Loving Kindness
May you be safe from Inner and Outer Dangers
May you be well in Body and Mind
May you be at Ease and Happy.

INTRODUCTION

This book is offered in gratitude to the philosophy of veganism and conscious eating. The two of us have been inspired at different times and in different ways to adopt and appreciate this alternative lifestyle and make changes to our old habits. It has been a slow process and a journey of immense learning. Through this book, we hope you will share some parts of our journey...

IS THIS BOOK FOR YOU?

- Are you trying to adopt healthier eating habits?
- Are you confused about what to eat and conflicting dietary advice?
- Do you run out of ideas about how to make healthy food exciting and tasty for your family?
- Do you want to lose weight, but find it difficult to stop eating?
- Do you want to adopt a lifestyle that can prevent cancer and diabetes, or lower your cholesterol, sugar levels, and blood pressure?
- Are you allergic to gluten or lactose?
- Has your doctor's advice to eliminate oil from your diet left you confused?
- Do you want to reduce your carbon footprint and eat sustainably?
- Are you a new vegan wondering how to replace cheese and milk in your favourite recipes?
- Are you an animal lover toying with veganism for ethical reasons?

If you answered yes to any of the above, then this book is for you.

WHY THIS BOOK?

This book was the result of discovering amazing and delicious whole, plant-based, and gluten-free foods. This discovery, with the additional benefit of weight-loss and well-being, is something we wanted to share with the world. We felt that this knowledge of how to make healthy food tasty must reach the masses, so that others who are on the path to health and conscious eating can partake in our good gastronomic fortune!

We often saw people struggle with making healthy food taste good. People who, in all earnestness, started a journey towards eating healthy often got bored with their limited repertoire of recipes. They sought the variety and stimulation available in restaurants. This inevitably led them to cheat on their health targets, as it is hard to find healthy options in restaurants. They ended up discouraged and disheartened about their chances of achieving their health goals.

We identified the most popular cuisines for eating out, picked the ones that we had some experience with, and attempted to bring this delicious food into your home.

WHAT THIS BOOK OFFERS

This book presents 108 recipes (we love this cosmic number). There are two menus presented for each cuisine and each menu offers nine dishes – a beverage, a starter, a soup, two salads, two mains, a side dish, and a dessert. This is to help you plan a party, catering wholesome foods for your friends and family. On regular days, you can pick and choose dishes and mix and match whatever takes your fancy. There are also 18 recipes to replace the dairy and sugar, and some basic recipes that are used frequently in this style of cooking. Apart from the fact that all our dishes are whole, plant-based, dairy-free, oil-free, sugar-free, and gluten-free, we have also taken care to include many dishes that are soy-free, nut-free, grain-free, and raw dishes too. This is to accommodate different eating preferences and personal choices.

We have re-introduced some of our planet's traditional and ancient grains like various types of millets available in India and abroad, which are highly nutritious and gluten-free. Millets are less resource-intensive and naturally hardy plants, so they are grown largely without irrigation or the use of chemicals and pesticides.

We have included a wide array of dishes that can be made in any kitchen anywhere in the world with everyday ingredients. In our testing phase, our volunteers reported that they found most of the ingredients at home in regular use. Others were easily available in stores. Some of the specialty cuisines might require some interesting food shopping which will enable you to widen your repertoire.

HOW TO USE THIS BOOK?

You will find some of your old favourites here with healthy, alternative recipes and cooking techniques. You will also find some completely new dishes. The old will comfort you and the new will challenge you. We encourage you to experiment, explore, and adapt it to suit your tastes and create your own new versions.

We have noticed a worrying trend in many urban homes. Due to the demands of fast-paced living, cooking has been relegated to the house help, or worse still, outsourced to corporations via fast food and packaged products. This book is an invitation to take back your power in the kitchen. This will put your family's health in your own hands. We believe that cooking is an act of self-care, an expression of love, a joyful bonding activity with your family or friends,

stimulation for your senses, a creative outlet, or just a relaxation for your mind. Discover what it means to you, and have fun trying out these recipes!

OUR HOPES AND BELIEFS

We hope that this book will show you that a whole, plant-based, vegan diet is abundant and delicious and not restrictive as it is often believed to be. The offerings of the plant kingdom are infinite, and the human ingenuity of cooking makes what we can eat endless in variety and flavour.

We believe that this is the future of our diets, consistent with the demands of modern society as also the needs of the Earth. Our planet simply cannot sustain the highly resource-intensive demands of animal agriculture for meat and dairy. Pesticides or GMO farming are also not sustainable in the long run as they come from a mindset that is against nature.

In fact, many farmers have demonstrated that organic farming is just as productive as conventional farming, and even more so over time. Conventional, large-scale, and industrial-style farming strips the soil of nutrients, kills its microbial life, and pollutes it with harmful chemicals and pesticides. Organic and natural methods of farming that are small scale and bio-diverse help to replenish the soil and build its natural health and immunity to resist disease and pests.

This book is not meant to be an imposition or a judgment on your present lifestyle or eating habits – whatever they might be. Allow your own awareness, personal experiences, and your body to guide you to make the right choices. Our only wish is to inspire you.

These recipes are offered to stimulate your senses to better appreciate the myriad, abundant offerings of the plant kingdom. This way of eating is beneficial to our health, the Earth, and other sentient beings with whom we share this planet.

Adopting this diet has benefitted us physically, emotionally, and spiritually. For us, it gives new meaning to the age-old Indian aphorism of *Vasudaiv Kutumbukam*: the whole world is our family!

We offer this book in service to our human and non-human family all over the world.

May you be healthy, may you be happy, may you be *Guilt Free*!

MALA AND NANDINI

10 WAYS TO MAKE YOUR FOOD MORE NUTRITIOUS

The whole plant-based diet calls for reverting to natural foods from plants in their whole (not refined) form. Hence, there is no food from animal sources. Also, we encourage organic methods of growing and not those artificially grown using chemical or biological interventions and harmful pesticides.

Food that is refined or processed in factories is less nutritious than whole foods. Refining processes like brown rice to white rice strip the grain of fibre and vital nutrients. When you extract oil from a seed or an olive, you take 100% fat and discard all the fibre. Hence, it's better to eat an olive or a peanut than the oil! Here are 10 basic guidelines to keep in mind for healthier eating.

1. From animal-based to plant-based.
2. From pesticide and chemical food to organic.
3. From refined grain (*maida*, *sooji*, white rice) to whole grain (millets, brown rice, etc.)
4. From refined sugar to whole (dates, raisins, and other dried fruits).
5. From juices to whole fruits and smoothies (on an empty stomach).
6. From extracted fats to the whole fats of nuts and seeds.
7. From peeled vegetables to unpeeled and whole.
8. Wash vegetables before cutting, and not after, to preserve nutrients.
9. From frying and over-cooking to blanching, steaming, sautéing without oil, and dry roasting.
10. From cooked meals to more fresh and raw foods.

KITCHEN REPLACEMENT CHART

FOOD/INGREDIENT	REPLACEMENT OPTIONS
BUTTER	Almond butter, avocado, cashew butter, peanut butter, and sesame butter.
BUTTERMILK	Buttermilk made from plant-based curd.
CHEESE	Cheese made from plant-based sources such as nuts, seeds, and nutritional yeast flakes.
CHOCOLATE	Cocoa powder, unprocessed cacao, or vegan dark chocolate.
CREAM	Cashew or other nut butters mixed with water and then ground.
CURD	Curd made from plant-based milks such as soy, peanut, rice etc.
EGGS	For baking – Ground flaxseeds whisked with water, soaked chia seeds, or mashed banana.
FRIED FOOD	Oil-free baked or roasted alternatives.
GHEE	Nuts, seeds, and legumes such as cashews, coconut, almonds, peanuts, and sesame seeds.
ICE CREAM	Plant-based milk or fruit ice creams sweetened with dried fruits.
MAYONNAISE	Oil-free cashew mayonnaise.
MEAT AND SEAFOOD	Soy nuggets and flakes, tofu, beans, ready-made meat replacers, and unripe jackfruit.
MILK	Plant-based milks including almond, coconut, cashew, oats, peanut, rice, sesame, and soy.
OIL	Whole nuts, seeds, and legumes such as cashews, coconut, peanuts, and sesame seeds.
PANEER	Tofu or 'soy paneer', and tofu marinated in cashew cream.
SALAD DRESSING	Oil-free salad dressings and chutneys.
SALT (IODIZED)	Himalayan, rock, or sea salt.
SOFT DRINKS	Water, lime juice with water, fruit smoothies, etc.
SUGAR, HONEY, AND ARTIFICIAL SWEETENERS	Dried fruits such as dates and raisins, stevia natural sweetener (use rarely).
TEA	Homemade infusions of herbs and spices, ready-made herbal teas.
WHITE FLOUR (MAIDA) AND BREAD	Whole grains like millets (e.g., *jowar*, *bajra*, *amaranth* and *ragi* etc.), brown rice.
WHITE RICE	Whole (unpolished) rice such as brown or red rice.

www.sharan-india.org

KITCHEN ESSENTIALS

A well-equipped kitchen is essential for *Guilt Free* cooking. Here is a checklist of some of the essential equipment and tools. This does not mean you have to go out and buy new gadgets and utensils tomorrow, but to start exploring how you can make your kitchen friendlier for healthier cooking in the coming months and years. It took us a couple of years to slowly phase out items that no longer suited our new cooking style.

EQUIPMENT

- Gas or electric hobs for cooking.
- Convection Oven with temperature settings (no microwave).
- Blender / Mixer for drinks and smoothies.
- Grinder for spices and nut butters etc.
- Food Processor for coarse grinding or fast grating / chopping.
- Juicer (for vegetable juices).

UTENSILS & TOOLS

- Good quality kitchen knives and a wooden chopping board are recommended.
- Use steel woks and pans or glass or ceramic dishes. Avoid non-stick, aluminium, and plastic as these release toxic chemicals into the food.
- A steamer would be an excellent addition for your oil-free cooking. If you have to buy just one new thing, let it be this (if you don't already have it).
- Mortar and pestle help to bring out rich flavours of spices and herbs when crushed fresh.
- Spiralizer is an optional addition that helps to make long noodles out of some raw vegetables.
- Other optional tools if you like to play in the kitchen are a julienne peeler, shaped cutters for pretty looking vegetables with curves and designs.

Left to Right: Steamer, Potato Masher, Julienne Cutter, Garlic Press, Whisk, Serrated Cutter, Melon Baller, Spiralizer, Tongs, Mortar and Pestle, Slicer.

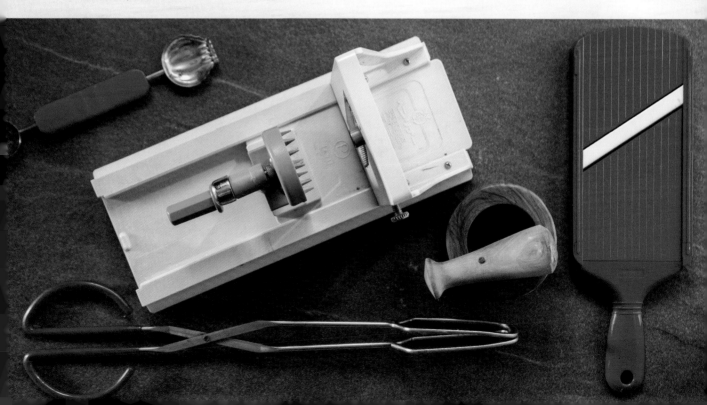

ITALIAN MENUS

Did you read *Eat Pray Love*? It is not surprising that Italy is often considered to be a foodie's paradise. On our last visit to Rome, we frequented a number of vegan restaurants. Most people think vegan food is boring so we put our thinking caps on to prove them wrong!

Here are our versions, all plant based, whole food, sugar and oil free put together as a full menu for you.

ITALIAN MENU 1

- CLEANSING BASIL AND CARROT JUICE
- WHOLESOME MINESTRONE SOUP
- FRESH TOMATO AND BASIL BRUSCHETTA
- ANTI-OXIDANT BEETROOT AND ORANGE SALAD
- FRESHLY TOSSED INSALATA MISTA
- WHEAT-FREE LASAGNA WITH CASHEW CREAM
- MUSHROOM AND ASPARAGUS RISOTTO
- WARM BROCCOLI AND PEPPERS FLAVOURED WITH ROSEMARY AND TOASTED ALMONDS
- SCRUMPTIOUS PISTACHIO GELATO

CLEANSING BASIL AND CARROT JUICE

The days we feast on fresh vegetable juices, we really look forward to the sweet tanginess of this fresh juice. Ginger is a great anti-inflammatory herb and basil adds an aromatic flavour.

SERVES 1

INGREDIENTS

» 4 medium-sized carrots
» ½˝ piece ginger
» 4-5 basil leaves
» 1 apple, optional

METHOD

1. Extract the juice of carrots and ginger. It should measure one glass. Separate the fibre.
2. Blend the basil leaves with a little juice till the leaves are liquidized. Add the remaining juice and blend again. Alternatively, you can mince the basil leaves and mix with the juice.
3. Serve chilled.

If you are not diabetic, you can add one apple for extra sweetness.

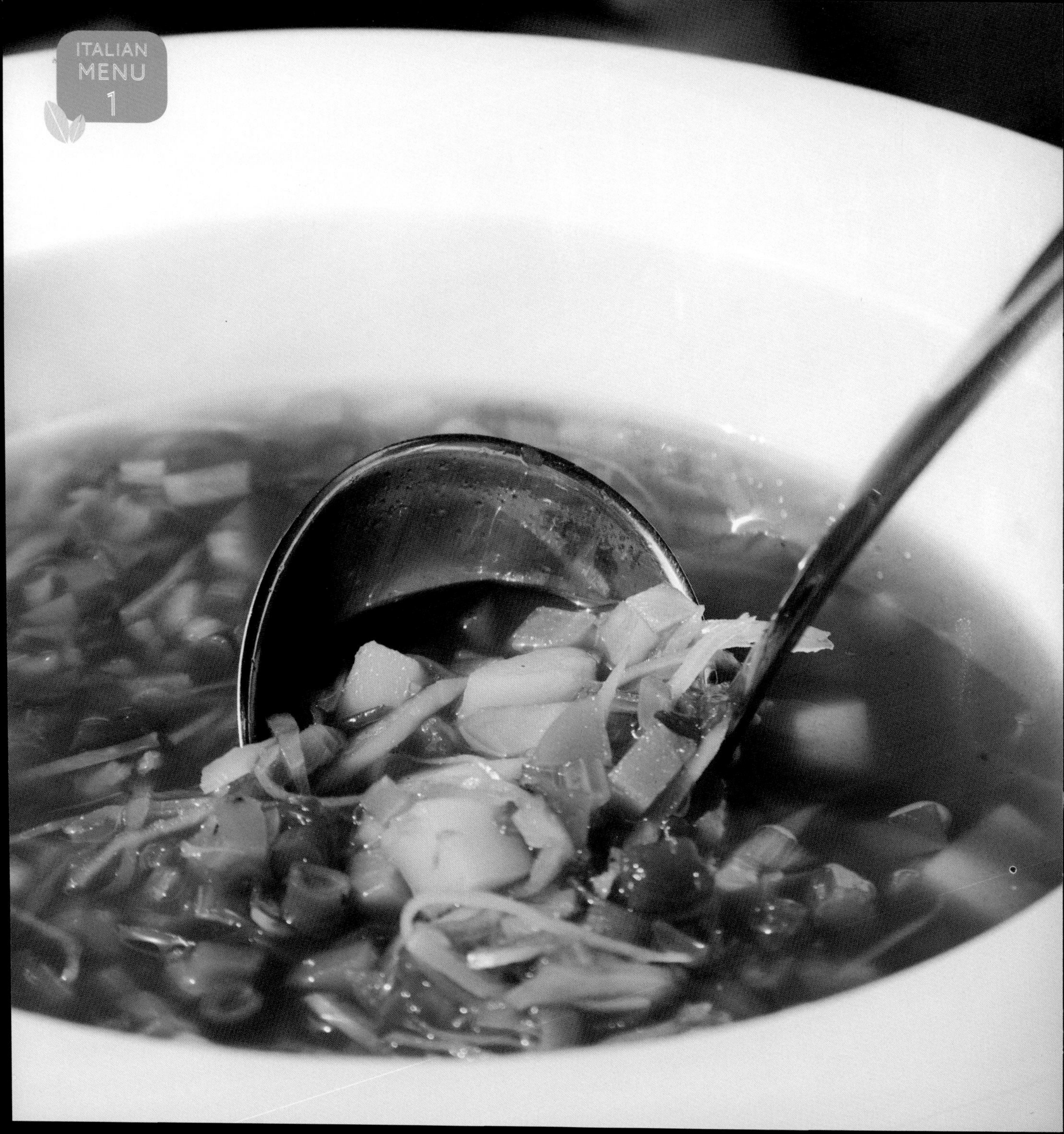

WHOLESOME MINESTRONE SOUP

Minestrone soup has been one of our all-time favourites, always wholesome and comforting. We love vegetables so this is really a soup for the soul.

SERVES 4-6

INGREDIENTS

- » 1 medium-sized onion, diced
- » 3 cloves garlic, diced
- » 1 potato, diced
- » 1 cup carrots, diced
- » 1 cup green beans, diced
- » ¼ green cabbage, shredded
- » 1 stick celery, diced
- » 6 tomatoes, diced
- » 2 cups vegetable stock (see pg. 219)
- » Salt and pepper to taste
- » 1 tsp oregano

METHOD

1. Add a little salt to the onion and allow it to release some water for 10 minutes.
2. Without oil, sauté the onion and garlic until golden.
3. Add the potato, carrots, beans, cabbage and celery; cook, covered, until the vegetables are soft.
4. Add the tomatoes and vegetable stock; bring to the boil.
5. Simmer till the vegetables are tender but not overcooked or mushy.
6. Add salt, pepper and oregano and simmer for 1-2 minutes. Remove from heat.
7. Serve the soup piping hot.

 Naturally sugary, sweet and crunchy, **CARROTS** are rich sources of anti-oxidants, vitamins, minerals and fibre. They are exceptionally rich in carotenes and vitamin A, which help prevent many types of cancer. They are among the highest alkalizing vegetables.

FRESH TOMATO AND BASIL BRUSCHETTA

This dish is served with oats crackers. I love the freshness of this recipe, allowing the tomatoes to fall off the sides as I bite into the fresh, crispy bruschetta!

SERVES 2-3

INGREDIENTS

For the oats crackers:
» 1 cup rolled oats
» Salt to taste
» ¼ cup water
» Black sesame seeds for sprinkling

For the tomato topping:
» 4 medium-sized ripe red tomatoes, diced
» 1 tbsp balsamic vinegar
» ½ tsp sea salt
» 1 bunch basil leaves
» 5 black olives
» 1 tsp balsamic vinegar reduction, optional

METHOD

1. **For the oats crackers**, mix the oats with salt. Add water to make a pulp.
2. Spread the pulp thinly on a baking tray lined with butter paper.
3. Bake at 200°C for 20 minutes till half-cooked. Remove from the oven.
4. With a sharp knife, make indentations for the cutting of the crackers. Sprinkle the crackers with black sesame seeds.
5. Bake for another 20 minutes, at the same temperature till slightly brown.
6. When cool, cut along the indentation into the required size.
7. **For the tomato topping**, toss all the ingredients well together.
8. Pile the crackers generously with this mixture just before eating.

Since the oats crackers are crumbly, they become soggy fast, so place the tomato topping only at the time of serving.

ANTI-OXIDANT BEETROOT AND ORANGE SALAD

A simple yet delicious salad! Not strictly Italian, but goes well with the menu.

SERVES 4

INGREDIENTS

- » 2 medium-sized beetroots, boiled, diced
- » 2 oranges, peeled, diced, pips removed
- » 1 medium-sized onion, peeled, diced
- » 1 tbsp lime juice
- » Salt to taste
- » A few mint leaves, for garnishing

METHOD

Mix all the ingredients in a salad bowl and sprinkle some mint leaves on top just before serving.

 BEETS are beneficial for cardiovascular health, they lower cholesterol and have anti-aging effects. Both the root, which contains a beneficial phytochemical, betaine and B-complex vitamins and the top leaves that are rich in vitamin C and carotenoids are good for our skin and vision.

FRESHLY TOSSED INSALATA MISTA

For this salad we usually use up whatever veggies we can find in our fridge, so don't restrict yourself to the ingredients below. The more the merrier but make sure the ingredients are fresh and the colours look vibrant.

SERVES 4

INGREDIENTS

- » 1 cup beans, carrots and broccoli, chopped
- » ½ cucumber, chopped
- » 2 tomatoes, sliced
- » ½ head of lettuce (romaine or iceberg)
- » 8 cherry tomatoes, halved
- » ¼ cup corn kernels
- » 1 apple, crisp, sliced
- » 2 tbsp black olives, sliced
- » ¼ cup almonds, roughly chopped
- » 1 tbsp cucumber / watermelon seeds

For the ginger and date dressing:
- » 1 tbsp ginger juice, fresh
- » 3 tbsp date paste (see pg. 218)
- » 1 tbsp lime juice
- » A pinch of salt

METHOD

1. Lightly steam the cup of mixed vegetables for 5 minutes and set aside to cool.
2. Once cooled, toss all the ingredients together making sure the colours of the salad look vibrant. Adjust any of the ingredients as you please.
3. **For the ginger and date dressing**, mix all the ingredients together and pour onto the salad just before serving.

Be careful not to stir the salad too much or mix the dressing too early as it makes the lettuce wilt. It's best done just before serving.

WHEAT-FREE LASAGNA WITH CASHEW CREAM

When we created this recipe and found that it was popular with kids, we realized we'd hit the jackpot. Everyone loves it!

SERVES 4

INGREDIENTS

» 2 potatoes, boiled
» 1 zucchini, thinly sliced lengthwise
» 2 carrots, thinly sliced lengthwise
» 1 eggplant, long, thinly sliced lengthwise
» Salt to taste
» A pinch of pepper and oregano
» Tomato milanese sauce (see pg. 219)
» Savoury cashew cream (see pg. 215)

METHOD

1. Layer a rectangular baking dish with potatoes, zucchini, carrots and eggplant lengthways so that they look like lasagna sheets.
2. Sprinkle some salt, pepper and oregano.
3. Spread a layer of tomato milanese sauce on top and then a layer of savoury cashew cream.
4. Repeat the layering till all the vegetables are used up.
5. Top with a small amount of tomato milanese sauce and a light layer of savoury cashew cream. Bake in the oven at 200°C for 40 minutes.
6. Serve hot.

MUSHROOM AND ASPARAGUS RISOTTO

Cooking risotto with brown rice needs a little adjustment, but once you get the hang of it, it makes a great wholesome dish on its own. Just remember to keep it moist, as we are not using any butter or olive oil.

SERVES 4

INGREDIENTS

» 2 cups brown rice
» 1 medium-sized onion, diced
» 2 cloves garlic, diced
» 1 cup vegetable stock (see pg. 219)
» 100 gm button mushrooms, sliced
» 3 sticks asparagus, chopped
» 6 cherry tomatoes, halved
» Salt and pepper to taste
» A few olives, sliced
» 1 tsp apple cider vinegar
» 1 sprig parsley

METHOD

1. Soak the brown rice for 2 hours in water. Throw out the soaking water and add 3 cups of fresh water; cook on low heat for 20 minutes till the water has evaporated and the rice is half done.
2. In a wok, sauté the onions and garlic without oil, until soft and transparent.
3. Now add the rice, stock, vegetables and salt and pepper to taste; cook on low heat for another 10 minutes or till the rice is fully cooked and the vegetables are still crunchy.
4. It's ok for the risotto to feel a little sticky, as it will remain moist.
5. Remove from heat. Add the sliced olives and the apple cider vinegar. Serve hot, garnished with a parsley sprig.

If you can't find apple cider vinegar, you can use any other natural vinegar like rice vinegar, etc. Please avoid synthetic vinegars.

WARM BROCCOLI AND PEPPERS FLAVOURED WITH ROSEMARY AND TOASTED ALMONDS

Broccoli and peppers when put together create an eclectic taste and texture. This recipe is as nutritious as it is delicious.

SERVES 4

INGREDIENTS

» 2 cups broccoli florets
» 1 red pepper
» 1 yellow pepper
» 2-3 cloves garlic, sliced into fine rounds
» A handful of bean sprouts or *mung* sprouts
» 1 sun-dried tomato, sliced
» 2 tbsp balsamic reduction
» 1 sprig fresh rosemary or ½ tsp dried rosemary
» Salt to taste
» ½ tsp freshly cracked black pepper
» A few almonds, sliced, toasted

METHOD

1. Steam the broccoli florets in a steamer for 5 minutes retaining the bright green colour.
2. Grill both the peppers in an open fire or in an oven grill at 220°C for 15 minutes on one side and 10 minutes on the other side. The skin of the peppers should be browned (not blackened) and flesh half cooked.
3. Bake the garlic in the oven simultaneously till brown and crisp.
4. Cool, de-seed and chop the peppers into 1″ squares.
5. Mix the broccoli, red and yellow peppers, bean sprouts and sun-dried tomato with the balsamic reduction, rosemary and salt; grill for 5 minutes.
6. Remove from grill and sprinkle with the cracked black pepper, baked garlic and toasted almond flakes just before serving.

If you don't find balsamic reduction in the stores, you can boil and reduce the normal balsamic to a thick consistency.

SCRUMPTIOUS PISTACHIO GELATO

'Gelato' or ice-cream is a favourite with the Italians. Thanks to plant-based milks, vegans too can enjoy this sweet treat. We use spinach to get a stronger green colour, which is a natural and healthy way to achieve this.

SERVES 4

INGREDIENTS

- » ½ cup unshelled raw pistachios
- » ½ cup almonds
- » 8 baby spinach leaves
- » 1½ cups water
- » 4 tbsp date paste (see pg. 218)
- » A pinch of salt
- » 1 tbsp raw pistachios, sliced for garnishing

METHOD

1. Steam the spinach and cool.
2. Purée the steamed spinach to a very smooth paste; set aside.
3. In a blender, grind the pistachios and almonds with 1 cup water. Add ½ cup more water, if required, to achieve a thick-pouring consistency.
4. Now add the date paste and blend together again.
5. Add the puréed spinach and a tiny pinch of salt; blend again.
6. Put into a container for the freezer and set in the fridge for 4 hours.
7. Take it out, stir the whole mixture and set again for 6 hours or overnight.
8. When set, scoop it out and garnish with some chopped pistachios before serving.

ITALIAN MENU 2

- AROMATIC PUMPKIN SMOOTHIE
- CHUNKY GAZPACHO SOUP
- STUFFED MUSHROOMS WITH GARLIC, TOMATOES AND OATS
- GREEN SALAD WITH AVOCADOS, WALNUTS AND ORANGES
- HIGH PROTEIN THREE BEAN SALAD
- SPINACH GNOCCHI WITH PUMPKIN SAUCE
- SURPRISING ZUCCHINI NOODLES WITH PRIMAVERA SAUCE
- GRILLED ITALIAN VEGETABLE MEDLEY WITH PESTO SAUCE
- WICKED CHOCOLATE AND ORANGE MOUSSE

AROMATIC PUMPKIN SMOOTHIE

This smoothie is creamy and light. We often use it as an afternoon indulgence for those sugar cravings. In the winter also, it is a comforting drink due to the spices.

SERVES 2

INGREDIENTS

- » 1 glass almond milk (see pg. 212)
- » 1 cup orange pumpkin, steamed, cooled
- » 1 ripe banana
- » 2 tbsp sweet raisins or 4 soft-pitted dates, preferably soaked
- » ½ tsp organic vanilla extract / powder
- » ¼ tsp ginger, minced
- » A pinch of clove powder
- » ¼ tsp cinnamon powder
- » A pinch of nutmeg powder
- » ½ glass ice

METHOD

1. Put all the ingredients in a blender except ice.
2. Blend until smooth. Add the ice if you like your drinks chilled; blend again.
3. Pour into a tall glass and serve sprinkled with cinnamon powder.

CHUNKY GAZPACHO SOUP

On a hot summers day if you don't feel like eating a cooked meal, this raw soup is the best antidote for the heat. It is filling, delicious and full of goodness. We call it a liquid salad and have made it a little extra tangy and spicy.

SERVES 4-6

INGREDIENTS

» 1 cucumber, roughly chopped
» 8 tomatoes, roughly chopped
» ½ green bell pepper, roughly chopped
» ½ red bell pepper, roughly chopped
» ½ stick celery, roughly chopped
» ½ red onion, roughly chopped
» 2 tbsp green coriander leaves
» 2 cloves garlic
» 1 tbsp apple cider vinegar
» A few drops of Tabasco sauce
» Salt and cracked black pepper to taste
» A sprig of mint

METHOD

1. Pack the vegetables in the food processor and blend until the vegetables are chunky allowing the juice from the tomatoes to create the base of the soup.
2. Splash a generous amount of apple cider vinegar and Tabasco sauce; stir well.
3. Add salt and cracked black pepper.
4. Serve chilled with an ice-cube in each bowl and garnished with a mint sprig.

STUFFED MUSHROOMS WITH GARLIC, TOMATOES AND OATS

Large mushrooms are not always available off-season in India, so we made this with button mushrooms. They are easy to pop into your mouth and wonderful as finger foods for parties instead of the regular fried stuff!

SERVES 4

INGREDIENTS

» 8 large button mushrooms
» 4 tomatoes, ½ cm of the top and bottom sliced off to form 8 caps, remaining tomato diced
» 1 onion, finely diced
» 2 cloves garlic, finely diced
» 1 tbsp oats
» 1 tbsp green coriander leaves, chopped
» Salt and black pepper to taste
» ½ diced green chilli, optional
» A pinch of oregano

METHOD

1. Destem the mushrooms and dice the stems keeping the heads whole.
2. Without oil, sauté the onion, garlic and diced tomatoes. When soft, add the diced mushroom stalks and salt to release the water.
3. Add the oats and cook until the mixture forms a paste.
4. Add the green coriander leaves, salt, black pepper, green chilli and oregano; cook for 30 seconds. Remove from heat and set aside to cool.
5. Lay the mushroom heads upside down and heap with the oats mixture as a stuffing. Top each with a tomato cap.
6. Place the mushrooms in a frying pan with a lid. Sprinkle some water and cover with a tight lid so it cooks in its own steam. Put heat on low and cook for 5 minutes or until the tomato tops are mildly cooked.
7. Serve hot, garnished with fresh green coriander leaves.

GREEN SALAD WITH AVOCADOS, WALNUTS AND ORANGES

Oil-free dressings are a new discovery for us. It has been really exciting to create new tastes and textures using whole seeds instead of oil.

SERVES 4

INGREDIENTS

» ½ head of ice-berg or any other lettuce, washed, dried, leaves torn
» 2 medium-sized / 1 large ripe avocado, 1 chopped, 1 mashed
» ½ cup orange segments, peeled, diced, pips removed
» ½ cup walnut halves, toasted
» 6 cherry tomatoes

For the orange and sesame dressing:
» 6 tbsp fresh orange juice
» 1 tsp lime juice
» 2 tsp white sesame seeds, toasted
» Salt to taste

METHOD

1. Mix the mashed avocado with the lettuce leaves giving a creamy coating to the leaves.
2. Add the chopped avocado, orange segments, walnuts and cherry tomatoes to the lettuce.
3. **For the orange and sesame dressing,** mix all the ingredients together and pour over the salad just before serving.

While fruit juices are not recommended for diabetics, a little bit in a salad dressing to substitute oil is allowed.

HIGH PROTEIN THREE BEAN SALAD

If you eat salads as a complete meal like we do, you will sometimes need something a little more filling. This is where the salad below works as a meal on its own for us. You can use any variety of beans according to availability.

SERVES 4

INGREDIENTS

» ½ cup red kidney beans, soaked overnight in double the amount of water
» ½ cup garbanzo beans or chickpeas, soaked overnight in double the amount of water
» ½ cup black-eyed beans, soaked for 1 hour before cooking
» 1 onion, diced
» 2 tomatoes, diced
» ½ cucumber, diced
» 3 tbsp lime juice
» Salt to taste
» ½ tsp green chillies, chopped for garnishing
» Green coriander leaves, chopped for garnishing

METHOD

1. Boil the beans separately – kidney beans and chickpeas for 30 minutes each till fully cooked but still firm.
2. Boil the black-eyed beans for 20 minutes till fully cooked but still firm.
3. Cool the beans and then toss with all the remaining ingredients in a salad bowl.
4. Serve garnished with green chillies (if you want that extra spark) and green coriander leaves.

Boiled beans can be added to any salad to make it filling. The high fibre gives satiety.

The gnocchi does not require much boiling, as it will disintegrate if kept in water for too long. Take it out within seconds.

SPINACH GNOCCHI WITH PUMPKIN SAUCE

We LOVE gnocchi and thus worked really hard to get this recipe right.
Hope you'll like it!

SERVES 4

INGREDIENTS

For the gnocchi:
» 2 large potatoes, halved
» 5-6 spinach leaves
» 1 tbsp cornflour
» Salt to taste

For the pumpkin sauce:
» 250 gm pumpkin, roughly chopped with skin
» ½ onion, diced
» 1 clove garlic, diced
» 2 stalks spring onions, head and stem chopped separately
» ¼ cup vegetable stock (see pg. 219)
» Salt and black pepper to taste
» 1 tsp rosemary, fresh or dried
» A few fresh sprigs of rosemary for garnishing

METHOD

1. Steam the potatoes for 10-12 minutes or till done.
2. Also steam the pumpkin pieces for 10 minutes. If you have a double stacking steamer, this can be done simultaneously.
3. Blanch the spinach leaves for 1 minute or steam for 4-5 minutes till wilted and soft.
4. Cool and make a purée of the wilted spinach in a grinder.
5. Mash the potatoes with the spinach purée and add the cornflour and salt.
6. Form little egg-shaped gnocchi balls with your hands and set aside.
7. **For the pumpkin sauce**, sauté the onion, garlic and heads of the spring onions.
8. Blend the steamed pumpkin with the onion mixture.
9. Add the vegetable stock and blend until smooth
10. Add salt, black pepper and rosemary. Cook for a few seconds, on low heat, to allow the fragrance of the rosemary to come through. Set aside.
11. Drop the gnocchi into a pan of boiling water.
12. When the gnocchi surfaces up in a few seconds, remove with a slotted spoon to drain out the water and lay it in your serving bowl.
13. Pour the pumpkin sauce over the gnocchi.
14. Serve garnished with fresh sprigs of rosemary or red bell pepper as shown.

SURPRISING ZUCCHINI NOODLES WITH PRIMAVERA SAUCE

Whenever we make these noodles in our retreats, it takes peoples' breath away. It just looks so beautiful! It's one of our favourite juicy raw dishes.

SERVES 4

INGREDIENTS

» 1 large zucchini
» 4 tomatoes, diced
» 1 tbsp balsamic vinegar
» Salt and black pepper to taste
» 8 black olives, whole
» A handful of whole basil leaves

METHOD

1. Put the zucchini through a spiralizer to create the noodles. (See image below on the left.) Alternatively, thinly slice the zucchini lengthways and fold over to cut thin, long strips creating the noodle effect. (See images below centre and right.)
2. Blend half the tomatoes into purée. Add to the rest of the diced tomatoes.
3. Add the balsamic vinegar, salt, black pepper, olives and basil leaves to the tomato mixture.
4. Lay the zucchini noodles on a dish and pour the primavera sauce over just before serving.

GRILLED ITALIAN VEGETABLE MEDLEY WITH PESTO SAUCE

When raw veggies become a bit monotonous for us non-raw foodies, we like to balance it with this delicious grilled vegetable dish. You can even keep it in your fridge and use it as a topping with crackers for when you need a snack!

SERVES 4

INGREDIENTS

For the pesto sauce:
» ½ cup cashew nuts
» ½ cup pine nuts
» 2 cups basil leaves
» Salt to taste

For the grilled vegetables:
» ½ zucchini
» ½ red pepper, cut into 8 pieces
» ½ yellow pepper, cut into 8 pieces
» ½ long eggplant, sliced
» 1 onion, peeled, quartered, separated
» 6 cloves garlic, whole
» 1 tsp mixed herbs

METHOD

1. **For the pesto sauce**, blend all the ingredients together with ¼ cup water to make a paste. Adjust the taste to your liking.
2. **For the grilled vegetables**, spread all the vegetables in a baking dish. Sprinkle salt and fold 2 tbsp of pesto sauce into the vegetables for moisture.
3. Grill at 220°C for 15 minutes or till starting to brown.
4. Then turn over the vegetables to allow the other side to cook. If too dry, brush some more pesto on the vegetables and grill for another 10 minutes till starting to brown.
5. Make sure the vegetables are moist enough with the pesto dressing.
6. Sprinkle with mixed herbs and serve.

WICKED CHOCOLATE AND ORANGE MOUSSE

This dish is the healthier version of the classic and is quite delightful. The orange rind gives it a refreshing flavour and masks the tofu quite well.

SERVES 4

INGREDIENTS

» 250 gm silken firm tofu
» 10-15 soft-pitted dates (adjust sweetness)
» 2-3 tbsp dark cocoa powder, adjust to taste
» 1 tsp orange rind, grated
» 1 sprig of mint

METHOD

1. Take a little tofu and blend with dates and cocoa powder.
2. Add the remaining tofu and blend again till completely smooth.
3. Taste for sweetness and if you require more, add more date paste (see pg. 218).
4. Add the orange rind and pulse for 10 more seconds. Allow some bits of rind to remain, as this will add some zing to the bite.
5. Scoop into small or tall tumblers and garnish with a little rind.
6. Chill in the fridge till ready to eat.
7. Add a sprig of mint before serving, if you like.

For a soy-free treat, replace the tofu with a ripe avocado. We like this even more than tofu when avocados are in season.

THAI MENUS

Vegetarian food in Thai restaurants can sometimes be tricky due to the ingredients. We have converted some of our favourite recipes using entirely vegan sauces so that you can enjoy the taste of restaurant-style food cooked in your own kitchen.

THAI MENU 1

- CLEAR COCONUT CHIA COOLER
- MUSHROOM AND YOUNG COCONUT TOM YUM SOUP
- SPICY TRI-COLOURED TIERED SALAD
- RAW PAPAYA SALAD
- SMOKED EGGPLANT WITH MINT AND CASHEW
- VEGETABLE GREEN COCONUT CURRY
- GRILLED GINGER TOFU WITH TERIYAKI SAUCE
- STIR-FRY POK CHOY WITH SHITAKE MUSHROOM
- REFRESHING ICE KASANG

CLEAR COCONUT CHIA COOLER

A simple and refreshing drink, the clear coconut chia cooler is full of natural goodness. This drink is high on Omega 3 from chia seeds which are good fats.

SERVES 2

INGREDIENTS

» 1 glass tender coconut water
» 2 tbsp young coconut meat
» ½ tsp chia seeds
» Ice as required

METHOD

1. In 1 cup coconut water, soak the chia seeds for 10 minutes till they absorb the liquid and are swollen.
2. Blend the remaining coconut water and chia seeds together with ice.
3. The little creamy bites of the floating coconut meat, gives it a nice texture.

MUSHROOM AND YOUNG COCONUT TOM YUM SOUP

In this version of Tom Yum soup we've used the coconut water as the base. The complete name is Tom Yum Hed Kap Ma Prow On, if you ever need to use it in Thailand!

SERVES 4

INGREDIENTS

» 2 fresh or dried oyster mushrooms (if available you can use enoki or shitake mushrooms also)
» 4 button mushrooms, quartered
» 4 cups tender coconut water
» 1 coconut, young, white meat removed and sliced into approx. 8 pieces of 2 x 1″
» 1 tsp galangal, roughly chopped
» 3 kaffir lime leaves, roughly crushed
» 1 stick lemongrass, roughly crushed
» 1 tomato, cut lengthways into 8 slices
» 1 spring onion, cut into 1″ length
» ½ cup lime juice
» ½ tsp dried red chilli flakes
» 1 green chilli, sliced into thin rounds
» Salt to taste
» A dash of soy sauce
» 1 tbsp green coriander leaves, chopped

METHOD

1. If using dried mushrooms, soak them in water for 4 hours. Then chop into large bite-size pieces.
2. Boil the coconut water along with galangal, kaffir lime leaves, lemongrass and mushrooms.
3. Add the tomato and spring onion. Cook for 1 minute and turn off the heat.
4. Add the lime juice, dried red chilli flakes, green chilli, salt, soy sauce and the coconut flesh.
5. Serve garnished with a green chilli or chopped green coriander leaves.

If you do not have enough coconut water, you can replace 1-2 cups with vegetable stock.

SPICY TRI-COLOURED TIERED SALAD

This salad is very pleasing to the eye and tastes delicious especially when you mix the dressing in. We like to call it 'Thai coleslaw' because you can eat lots of it!

SERVES 4

INGREDIENTS

» ¼ red cabbage, cut into thin strips
» 1 medium-sized carrot, julienned
» 1 medium-sized raw mango, julienned

For the dressing:
» ½ red chilli, coarsely chopped
» 1 tbsp tamarind paste
» 1 tbsp date paste (see pg. 218)
» 3 tsp coconut cream
» 2 tsp peanuts, roasted, coarsely crushed
» A slice of coconut, roasted, optional for garnishing

METHOD

1. On a serving plate, layer the red cabbage, carrot and raw mango to create a colourful tier.
2. Mix all the ingredients of the dressing and pour over the tiered vegetables and serve chilled.
3. Garnish with a slice of roasted coconut.

CABBAGES are among the world's healthiest foods, belonging to the cruciferous family. Red cabbage is extra beneficial as the red pigment comes from natural phyto-chemicals. Their sharp flavour is the result of sulfur-based compounds. They have anti-cancer and anti-inflammatory properties.

RAW PAPAYA SALAD

The most popular salad in Thailand had to be included in our book. When we make it for our family and friends, it's always a sell out!

SERVES 4

INGREDIENTS

½ raw papaya, julienned
1 tsp chilli flakes
2 limes, cut into half
2 tbsp lime juice
1 green chilli, chopped
1 red chilli, chopped
2 tbsp mint leaves
4 kaffir lime leaves, crushed
2 tbsp green coriander leaves
Salt to taste
2 tsp raisin paste (see pg. 218)
1 medium-sized onion, sliced
2 medium-sized tomatoes, sliced
lengthways into 10 pieces

For the garnishing:
4 mint sprigs
½ cup peanuts, roasted

METHOD

1. Put the papaya juliennes in a bowl
2. In a mortar and pestle, pound all the other ingredients together except salt, raisin paste, half the onion slices and tomatoes to just release the juices and fragrances. It should take around 2-3 minutes. Don't overdo it and make a mash.
3. Add the salt, raisin paste, remaining onions and tomato slices.
4. Place on a serving dish and create a mound.
5. Serve garnished with roasted peanuts and fresh mint leaves.

PAPAYA contains more vitamin C than oranges or lemons. It is an immunity booster, anti-inflammatory, anti-parasitic and has analgesic properties. It is popular in traditional medicines. Its soluble dietary fibre helps regularize bowel movements. It is amongst the highly alkalizing fruits.

To roast the sliced garlic, bake at 200°C for approximately 10 minutes till browned and crispy.

SMOKED EGGPLANT WITH MINT AND CASHEW

This is a traditional recipe from the northern Lanna region of Thailand, and uses eggplant in an unusual way. This interesting and easy-to-make dish is always a hit at parties.

SERVES 4

INGREDIENTS

For the eggplant:
2 long eggplants
½ cup lime juice
1 tsp raisin paste (see p. 218)
Salt to taste
1 red chilli, split into half

For the topping:
½ onion, sliced
2 tbsp cashew nuts, roasted
2 tbsp mint, fresh, chopped
2 tbsp green coriander leaves, chopped
½ -1 tsp green chillies, chopped
½ tsp dried red chilli flakes
1 tbsp crispy roasted garlic (p. 70, Chef's tip)

METHOD

1. Smoke the eggplants on open fire until soft and cooked. Alternatively, grill on high heat till charred. Remove the charred skin.
2. Test with a fork to check if it is cooked through without being too soft.
3. Place the long eggplants on a rectangular dish lengthways and slice into 3 pieces each.
4. Whisk together the lime juice, raisin paste and salt and pour over the eggplants.
5. Prepare the salad by sprinkling all the toppings over it.
6. Serve garnished with a half split red chilli.

VEGETABLE GREEN COCONUT CURRY

Only when we first made this curry paste fresh did we realize the number of ingredients that go into it, and why it was so delicious. This had to be included as a must-have.

SERVES 4

INGREDIENTS

» ½ medium-sized carrot, sliced
» 4 cauliflower florets or ½ head
» 1 stick long bean, chopped
» 4 baby onions
» 8 medium-sized button mushrooms, quartered
» ½ cup Thai brinjals (optional)
» 4 cups thick coconut milk (first press see pg. 213)
» 6 kaffir lime leaves
» 1 red bell pepper, chopped
» 4 strips of lemongrass sticks, about 3-4″ each
» 2 whole red chillies, split lengthways
» Salt to taste

For the green curry paste:
» 2 green chillies
» 4 kaffir lime leaves
» 1 tbsp lemongrass stick, sliced
» 1 tsp galangal, chopped
» 1 tsp coriander powder
» 2 tbsp garlic, chopped
» ¼ cup spring onions, sliced
» 5 black peppercorns
» ½ tsp roasted cumin powder

METHOD

1. **For the green curry paste**, blend all the ingredients together and cook in a pan or wok for about 7 minutes until you can smell the flavours emanating.
2. Add in the vegetables, starting with carrot, cauliflower, bean and onions. Cook for 2 minutes.
3. Add in the mushrooms and Thai brinjals (if using) and cook, covered, for 5-7 minutes keeping the vegetables crunchy.
4. Add in the thick coconut milk along with whole kaffir lime leaves, red pepper, lemongrass sticks and split red chillies.
5. Add salt, heat thoroughly making sure to turn off the heat before the mixture comes to the boil as it may tend to separate.
6. This is a fragrant curry. Enjoy it hot with brown or red rice.

GRILLED GINGER TOFU WITH TERIYAKI SAUCE

For some reason this recipe never fails to delight people. We think the blandness of the tofu is lifted with the tangy taste of the sauce.

SERVES 4

INGREDIENTS

» 1 packet silken firm tofu, sliced into 2 cm thick pieces
» 2 tbsp soy sauce
» 1 tbsp teriyaki sauce
» 1 tbsp ginger, grated
» ½ tsp date paste (see pg. 218)
» 2 tbsp greens of spring onions, chopped

METHOD

1. Place the tofu slices in a grill pan.
2. Combine the sauces, ginger and date paste and pour over the tofu.
3. Grill on high heat for 5 minutes.
4. Remove from grill and serve garnished with spring onion greens.

SOY is just a bean. There is a lot of controversy around it. It has been both praised and questioned a lot on various grounds. However, it has been eaten for centuries in South East Asia. It is neither extra beneficial, nor extra harmful just like any other bean. You wouldn't eat kidney beans everyday, nor is there any need to consume soy products everyday.

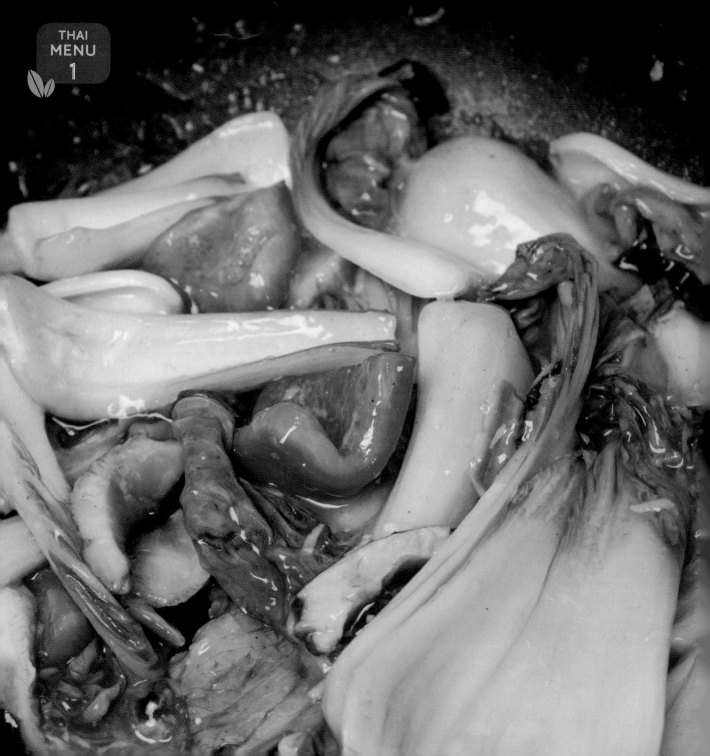

STIR-FRY POK CHOY WITH SHITAKE MUSHROOMS

A nice wholesome serving of greens, this should be prepared last and as close to serving as possible.

SERVES 4

INGREDIENTS

» 2 heads of pok choy, leaves separated, washed thoroughly
» 6 fresh or dried shitake mushrooms
» 1 tbsp garlic, chopped
» 1 red pepper, chopped
» 1 handful bean sprouts, optional

For the sauce:
» 1 cup vegetable stock (see pg. 219)
» 1 tsp cornflour

METHOD

1. If using dried mushrooms, soak in warm water for 6-8 hours or overnight. Slice the soaked mushrooms.
2. Dry fry the garlic in a wok for 3-4 minutes till brown. Add the mushrooms and stir-fry for another 3-4 minutes.
3. Add the pok choy and red pepper and stir-fry for 1-2 minutes.
4. **For the sauce**, whisk the vegetable stock and cornflour together and add to the vegetables. Add the bean sprouts (optional).
5. Stir until the sauce thickens. Remove from heat.
6. Serve immediately.

 GREEN LEAFY VEGETABLES are highly alkalizing and pack in all the essential nutrients and fibre with the best anti-oxidants and anti-inflammation properties from the plant world. They are the favourite food of the beneficial microorganisms that live in our gut and contribute to our digestive health.

REFRESHING ICE KASANG

This dessert is great when you seek respite from the hot and humid weather! The fresh fruit and coconut milk makes this a good replacement for any heavy creamy dessert.

SERVES 4

INGREDIENTS

» 2 cups of mixed diced fruit – watermelon, pomegranate, apple, crunchy pears, musk melon (any other crunchy fruits)
» ½ tsp raisin paste (see p. 218)
» 1 cup coconut milk (see p. 213)
» 1 kg crushed ice

METHOD

1. Place the crushed ice in a small serving bowl heaped like a pyramid.
2. Sprinkle the diced fruit on the ice in equal portions.
3. Mix the raisin paste and coconut milk with a whisk or fork.
4. Pour the coconut milk on the fruit pyramids.
5. Serve immediately.

THAI MENU 2

- AROMATIC LEMONGRASS TEA
- HOT AND SOUR VEGETABLE SOUP
- TOFU SATAY WITH PEANUT SAUCE
- MOST DELICIOUS LANNA GUAVA SALAD
- CRUNCHY LETTUCE POPIYA
- PINEAPPLE FRIED RICE
- PUMPKIN AND LOTUS STEM MASSAMAN CURRY
- BLANCHED SPINACH WITH BALSAMIC REDUCTION AND SESAME SEEDS
- TRADITIONAL SWEET MANGO AND STICKY RICE

AROMATIC LEMONGRASS TEA

Infusions are a great alternative to regular tea as they are not acidic and yet you can get the satisfaction of drinking a hot beverage. The fragrance of kaffir lime and the goodness of lemongrass will leave you refreshed.

SERVES 2

INGREDIENTS

» 2 cups water
» 1 stem of lemongrass, chopped, crushed to release fragrance
» 2 kaffir lime leaves, torn
» Stevia Natural Sweetener, optional

METHOD

1. Bring the water to the boil in a pot. Turn off the heat and add lemongrass and kaffir leaves as an infusion. Cover and brew for 5 minutes.
2. Sieve the tea and add stevia sweetener, if required, before serving.

HOT AND SOUR VEGETABLE SOUP

Indians love the Chinese hot and sour soup so here is a Thai version of it that's equally good. Use whatever veggies you find in your fridge.

SERVES 4

INGREDIENTS

» 2 long green beans, cut into 1½″-long pieces
» 1 onion, quartered
» 2 cups cauliflower florets
» ½ carrot, sliced
» 3 cups vegetable stock (see p. 219)
» 1 stick lemongrass, cut into 2″ long pieces
» ¼ cup tamarind juice
» 4 tbsp lime juice
» 2 tsp date or raisin paste (see p. 218)
» Salt to taste

For the sour curry paste:
» 6 kaffir lime leaves, finely chopped
» 1 tbsp galangal, sliced
» 2 garlic cloves
» 3 Thai red chillies, fresh
» 2 tbsp spring onions, chopped

METHOD

1. **For the sour curry paste**, pound or blend all the ingredients until smooth.
2. Boil the vegetable stock with the lemongrass over medium heat. Stir in the sour curry paste. Season with the tamarind juice, lime juice, salt, and raisin paste to obtain a balance of sour, salty and sweet.
3. Add all the vegetables and cook till crunchy and not too soft. This will take about 7-8 minutes in all.
4. Turn off the heat and let the soup sit for 5 minutes to absorb all the flavours.
5. Serve hot.

Traditionally satay is served on bamboo skewers. If you want to use skewers, handle the tofu with care as it tends to be crumbly. Insert the skewers after grilling to prevent breaking.

TOFU SATAY WITH PEANUT SAUCE

A Thai meal is not complete without satay. We have used tofu here but honestly some veggies on a stick could also make a great veg satay!

SERVES 4

INGREDIENTS

» 250 gm firm tofu
» 3 tbsp soy sauce
» 2 tbsp ginger, grated

For the peanut sauce:
» 1 cup peanut butter (see pg. 217)
» 2 tbsp lime juice
» 2 tbsp date paste (see p. 218)
» ½ tbsp garlic
» ½ tsp chilli powder
» Salt to taste

METHOD

1. Marinate the tofu with ginger and soy sauce for at least 4 hours.
2. Grill on both sides on high heat until brown. Remove from heat.
3. **For the peanut sauce,** prepare by blending all the ingredients together.
4. Serve with the tofu satay as an accompaniment.

This salad is again a recipe from Northern Thailand where the Burmese Lanna Kingdom had a great influence. At Dhara Devi this was our staple and we are so excited to be able to share this with you!

SERVES 4

INGREDIENTS

» 1 big Thai guava, julienned
» ½ cup tamarind paste
» 2 tomatoes, cut each into 8 long slices
» ½ onion, thinly sliced
» 1 tbsp roasted garlic (see pg. 70, Chef's tip)
» 2 spring onions, only the greens chopped to ½ cm pieces
» ½ cup mint leaves, chopped
» ¼ cup green coriander leaves, torn
» 1 red chilli, chopped into large pieces
» 1 green chilli, chopped into large pieces
» Salt to taste
» 1 head lettuce leaves
» 2 tbsp onions, finely chopped
» ½ cup cashew nuts, roasted

METHOD

1. Soak the tamarind for 4 hours in 1 cup warm water or enough water to cover.
2. Remove the skin and seeds by sieving it to get a paste. This will yield approximately ½ cup paste.
3. Fold the tamarind paste into the guava strips.
4. Add all the chopped vegetables to the salad bowl along with the guavas; mix well together.
5. On a serving dish, spread a bed of lettuce and lay the guava salad in the centre.
6. Garnish with pan-roasted onions, cashews and mint leaves.

Note: If Thai guava is not available use a mix of Indian guava and apple.

CRUNCHY LETTUCE POPIYA

Traditionally popiya is made of thin rice paper rolls. Here is our *Guilt Free* version which is scrumptiously crunchy, juicy and leaves you craving for more!

SERVES 4

INGREDIENTS

» 8 leaves of ice-berg lettuce
» ½ carrot, cut into 3″-long sticks
» ½ cucumber, cut into 3″-long sticks
» ½ yellow capsicum, cut into 3»-long sticks
» ½ red capsicum, cut into 3″-long sticks
» 1 tbsp lime juice
» Salt to taste
» 1 cup peanut sauce (see pg. 85)

METHOD

1. Squeeze some lime juice and salt over the vegetables and mix.
2. To make a parcel, place 4-5 vegetable sticks lengthways at the centre of a lettuce leaf.
3. Pour a tbsp of peanut sauce and fold the lettuce leaf over; secure with a toothpick.

PEANUTS are technically legumes, but they have almost all the qualities of other popular nuts. They are a good source of vegetarian protein essential for growth and development. Peanuts are an excellent source of resveratrol, a polyphenolic antioxidant with protective properties against cancer, heart disease, degenerative nerve disease and viral / fungal infections.

PINEAPPLE FRIED RICE

It's not recommended to mix fruit with carbs and other veggies but if you're willing to bend the rules, this recipe is delicious.

SERVES 4

INGREDIENTS

» 4 cups cooked brown rice
» 2 cups mixed, diced vegetables (carrots, beans, onions, corn, broccoli, red pepper)
» Salt to taste
» 1 tbsp soy sauce
» 1 cup sweet pineapple, diced
» ½ scooped pineapple shell

METHOD

1. Pan-fry all the vegetables together on low heat for approximately 10 minutes until you can smell the aroma.
2. Add the rice, salt and soy sauce; mix well together. Let it heat through and then add the pineapple; mix together.
3. Cover and let it sit for at least 10-15 minutes till ready to serve.
4. Use the scooped pineapple shell as your serving dish.
5. Heap the fried rice into the empty shell and decorate with a split red chilli.

Brown rice needs to be soaked for at least 2 hours and then cooked into 2.5 times water. It will take 20 minutes.

PUMPKIN AND LOTUS STEM MASSAMAN CURRY

A hard-to-find recipe, this quintessential Thai dish packs in ample nutrition and flavour. A sure hit at your next family dinner.

SERVES 4

INGREDIENTS

» 100 gm pumpkin, cut into large cubes
» 4 small eggplants, slit in the middle
» ½ lotus stem, sliced
» 6 baby corn, sliced lengthways
» 3 bay leaves
» 4 kaffir lime leaves
» 1 pod green cardamom
» 2 tbsp tamarind paste
» 1 tsp soy sauce
» 1 tsp raisin paste (see pg. 218)
» 2 cups coconut milk (see pg. 213)
» Salt to taste

For the massaman paste:
» 1-2 red chillies
» 1 tsp galangal, sliced
» 6″ lemongrass stalk, sliced
» 2 cloves garlic
» 3 spring onions, sticks
» 1 tbsp roasted coriander powder
» 1 tsp cumin powder
» ¼ tsp cloves or cinnamon, powdered
» 1 tsp crushed black peppercorns

METHOD

1. Steam the eggplants, lotus stem, baby corn and pumpkin in a steamer for 7 minutes till ¾th done and still firm.
2. **For the massaman paste**, pound or blend all the ingredients with a little water to form a smooth paste.
3. Sauté the paste with ½ cup water for 4-5 minutes until the aroma is released.
4. Add the steamed vegetables with bay leaves, kaffir lime leaves and green cardamom. Add a little water, if required, and cook covered on medium heat for 5 minutes till the spices have seeped into the vegetables.
5. Now add the tamarind paste, soy sauce, raisin paste, coconut milk and salt; stir gently.
6. Bring to the boil and remove from heat.
7. Serve hot garnished with split red chillies.

This dish stores well in the fridge if you have any leftovers as this allows all the flavours to merge well with the vegetables.

BLANCHED SPINACH WITH BALSAMIC REDUCTION AND SESAME SEEDS

This dish is not strictly Thai, but goes well with the menu and we love it. So we decided to include it here and share its goodness with you.

SERVES 4

INGREDIENTS

- » 250 gm spinach, washed, cleaned thoroughly
- » 3 tbsp balsamic vinegar reduced
- » 3 tbsp sesame seeds, toasted
- » Salt to taste

METHOD

1. Take a pan of boiling hot, salted water and blanch the spinach for a few seconds just to wilt them.
2. Remove from the water and spread the wilted leaves evenly on a plate, one at a time, forming a symmetrical pattern. Squeeze the leaves lengthways in order to even them out.
3. Pour the reduction over the leaves and sprinkle the toasted sesame seeds on top evenly.

TRADITIONAL SWEET MANGO AND STICKY RICE

This dessert is so popular that even Bangkok airport now sells it off the counter for salivating tourists to take home!

SERVES 4

INGREDIENTS

» 2 ripe mangoes, peeled, sliced into 2, seeds removed
» 1 cup cooked sticky rice
» 1 tbsp raisin paste (see p. 218)
» A pinch of salt
» Coconut cream for garnishing
» Sesame seeds for garnish, toasted

METHOD

1. Mix the sticky rice with the raisin paste and salt.
2. Pack a small bowl tightly with the rice and overturn the rice out on a plate.
3. Partly place the mango over the rice and pour the coconut cream. Sprinkle the sesame seeds over the entire dish.
4. Serve chilled.

MANGO is the king of fruits, not just in taste but health benefits too. It is rich in pre-biotic dietary fibre, minerals and anti-oxidants. It provides protection against cancer, resistance to infections and is heart healthy. It is rich in phytonutrients, carotenoids and polyphenols.

MEDITERRANEAN MENUS

From Greece to Turkey to Lebanon, the Mediterranean cuisine ranges far and wide. Often, the dips and breads are similar yet different, if you know what we mean!

MED MENU 1

- DELECTABLE FRUIT PARFAIT
- MEDITERRANEAN LENTIL AND CUMIN SOUP
- BEETROOT PINK TZATZIKI
- JUICY CHERRY TOMATOES AND BABY ONIONS IN TAHINI SAUCE
- RAINBOW SALAD WITH APPLE, MUSTARD DRIZZLE
- EGGPLANT MOUSSAKA WITH SPINACH, TOMATO AND CASHEW CREAM
- QUINOA MEDLEY
- STEAMED OKRA WITH TANGY SAUCE
- DELICIOUS DATE AND WALNUT HALWA

DELECTABLE FRUIT PARFAIT

This is our most favourite snack. It is completely healthy with lots of fruits and their colourful phytonutrients. Technically not a drink, but we could not resist putting this in the book. Since we do not advocate fruit as dessert, we put it at the beginning of a menu.

SERVES 2

INGREDIENTS

- » 1 cup papaya, chopped
- » 1 cup mango or strawberries, chopped
- » 1 cup banana, chopped
- » ½ cup kiwi fruit
- » A sprig of mint for garnishing

METHOD

1. Blend each fruit, separately, washing the jar in-between.
2. Arrange the fruit pulp in a fancy glass in 3-4 different coloured layers.
3. Decorate with a sprig of mint and serve chilled.

You can use any pulpy fruits. Anything watery or crunchy will not work. You can use strawberries, pitted cherries, blueberries or any other berries available.

MEDITERRANEAN LENTIL AND CUMIN SOUP

The Lebanese have taken our common dal and turned it into this interesting soup with lemon and cumin. We love the combination!

SERVES 4

INGREDIENTS

» 1 cup pink lentils (*masoor dal*)
» 4 cups water
» 2 juice of limes
» 1 tsp roasted cumin powder
» Salt to taste

METHOD

1. Boil the lentils with 3 cups water for 20 minutes or until cooked. Allow it to cool.
2. Add salt and process in the blender for approximately 3 minutes to make a smooth consistency.
3. Pour into a larger pan. Bring to the boil and add the remaining water to the pan. Heat thoroughly, if required.
4. Before serving, add lime juice and ½ tsp cumin powder; stir well.
5. Sprinkle the remaining cumin powder on top before serving.

 LENTILS are a great source of lean plant-based protein and are high in fibre. Therefore they can lower your cholesterol and help keep your arteries clean. They are also beneficial for gut health and help stabilize blood sugar.

BEETROOT PINK TZATZIKI

This pretty pink dish is so easy to make once you have the vegan curd.

SERVES 4

INGREDIENTS

» ½ medium-sized beetroot, grated
» 2 cups soy curd (see pg. 214)
» 1 pod garlic, crushed
» Salt to taste
» Black peppercorns, freshly crushed, to taste, optional
» ½ cup mint leaves, finely chopped

METHOD

1. Smoothen the curd with a whisk or in a blender.
2. Add the crushed garlic, salt and pepper, if using, and stir.
3. Finally stir in the mint leaves and beet and watch the curd turn pink.
4. Enjoy as a dip or as an accompaniment with crackers (see pg. 29) or crudités.

You can also do a green tzatziki using steamed spinach and blending it before mixing into the curd.

JUICY CHERRY TOMATOES AND BABY ONIONS IN TAHINI SAUCE

Crunchy red tomatoes with broken baby onions, this salad always makes a good snack. The tahini sauce is made from sesame seeds, one of the richest sources of calcium, 10 times more than dairy milk.

SERVES 4

INGREDIENTS

» 1 cup cherry tomatoes
» 1 cup baby onions, peeled
» 10 walnut halves
» ½ cup sprigs of parsley

For the dressing:
» 1 tbsp tahini (see pg. 217)
» 3 tbsp lime juice
» 1 clove garlic, grated
» 2 tbsp vegetable stock (see p. 219)
» Salt to taste

METHOD

1. Roast the onions in a pan on high heat with 2 tbsp vegetable stock. Cover and cook on medium heat for 5-7 minutes until the outer layers are brown and loose. Remove and keep aside to cool.
2. Mix the tomatoes and onions together. Use the back of a fork to crush the onions lightly so that the outer skin of the onions break away. Make sure they still retain their shape.
3. **For the dressing**, mix all the ingredients by whisking or blending together.
4. In a large salad bowl, combine the dressing with the vegetables and toss to evenly coat the dressing.
5. Serve garnished with walnuts and parsley.

RAINBOW SALAD WITH APPLE, MUSTARD DRIZZLE

The colours of this salad always take our breath away! Eating multi-hued vegetables provides a diversity of nutrients, and we encourage people to eat a rainbow of colours everyday.

SERVES 6

INGREDIENTS

- » 4 medium-sized tomatoes, sliced into rounds
- » 2 medium-sized carrots, grated
- » 100 gm pumpkin, grated
- » 2 yellow capsicum, chopped into long pieces
- » 2 cups spinach, chopped
- » 100 gm red cabbage, shredded
- » 100 gm green cabbage, shredded
- » 1 medium-sized beet, grated

For the dressing:
- » ¼ cup apple juice, fresh
- » 1 garlic pod, grated
- » ¼ tsp oregano, dried or freshly crushed
- » 6-8 basil leaves, crushed
- » 1 tbsp mustard sauce
- » 2 tbsp lime juice
- » Salt to taste

METHOD

1. Arrange all the vegetables in concentric circles like a rainbow starting with violet or purple in the centre.
2. **For the dressing**, whisk or blend all the ingredients together.
3. Drizzle the dressing over the salad just before serving.

EGGPLANT MOUSSAKA WITH SPINACH, TOMATO AND CASHEW CREAM

This is one of our most popular recipes. It never fails to impress whoever gets a taste of it! We make it look like a burger to give it another dimension.

SERVES 4

INGREDIENTS

» 2 large, round eggplants, sliced into ¾ cm-thick rounds
» 12 spinach leaves
» 2 large potatoes, boiled, sliced into ½ cm rounds
» 1 cup tomato milanese sauce (see pg. 219)
» 1 cup savoury cashew cream (see pg. 215)
» Salt to taste
» 2 tbsp crispy garlic (pg. 70)
» ½ cup green olives
» Sprigs of mint for garnishing

METHOD

1. Sprinkle some salt over the eggplants and let it rest for 30 minutes to release excess water.
2. Grill the eggplant slices on high heat, at 220ºC, for 15 minutes on each side till brown.
3. Blanch the spinach leaves in hot water for 5 seconds till just wilted.
4. In a serving dish, spread the eggplant slices to form the bottom layer.
5. Now add a layer of sliced potatoes and sprinkle some salt.
6. Take the wilted spinach and layer it next. Spread 1 tbsp of tomato milanese sauce followed by 1 tbsp of cashew cream.
7. Top it with another layer of eggplant. Repeat the process of layering as above ending with eggplant.
8. Garnish the moussaka with a little tomato sauce, cashew cream, roasted garlic, olives and sprigs of mint.

QUINOA MEDLEY

Quinoa is a nutritious seed used as a gluten-free grain with ancient origins in South America. It is so versatile and can be made in so many ways, we love it. Here is our version with lots of veggies and goodness!

SERVES 4

INGREDIENTS

- » 1 cup quinoa
- » 2 cups water
- » 2 tbsp onion, chopped
- » 1 clove garlic, chopped
- » 2 tbsp carrot, diced
- » 2 tbsp beans, chopped
- » ½ cup cherry tomatoes, halved
- » ½ yellow capsicum, diced
- » ½ red capsicum, diced
- » 1 tbsp mint leaves, chopped
- » 2 tbsp black olives, sliced
- » Salt to taste
- » ½ tbsp balsamic vinegar
- » 1 tbsp lime juice

METHOD

1. Cook the quinoa in 2 cups water in a covered pan for approximately 20 minutes until all the water is absorbed and the quinoa is soft.
2. Add ¼ tsp salt to the onion to allow it to sweat for 10 minutes. Without oil, sauté the onion and garlic until slightly brown. Add the carrots, beans and tomatoes.
3. When the carrots are half cooked, add in the yellow and red capsicum, mint and olives. Add salt and mix well; turn off the heat.
4. Add in the cooked quinoa and mix well again.
5. Before serving, stir in the balsamic vinegar, lime juice and adjust the salt.
6. Serve garnished with olives.

Quinoa can be substituted in this recipe by any of the indigenous millets like foxtail, kodo or proso.

STEAMED OKRA WITH TANGY SAUCE

This recipe won the first prize at a vegan potluck for its originality and simplicity. It is easy to make and delightful to eat!

INGREDIENTS

» 200 gm okra, washed, cleaned

For the sauce:
» 1 tsp garlic, crushed
» 1 tbsp teriyaki sauce
» 1 tbsp soy sauce
» 1 tbsp lime juice
» 1 tbsp balsamic vinegar
» 1 tbsp date paste (see pg. 218)
» A pinch of red chilli powder, crushed
» Salt to taste

METHOD

1. Blanch the whole okras in a pan of freshly boiled hot water with 1 tsp salt and stand for 1 minute till done.
2. **For the sauce**, mix all the ingredients with some salt by whisking with a fork.
3. Arrange the okra on a round plate and drizzle the sauce over the okra. Serve.

To retain the bright green colour of okra, add ¼ tsp baking soda to the hot water while blanching.

DELICIOUS DATE AND WALNUT HALWA

All our friends love this dessert at our dinner parties. It also works as a snack for those afternoon sweet cravings.

SERVES 4

INGREDIENTS

» 1 cup walnuts, shelled, raw, broken into chunky bits
» ½ cup almonds, roasted, roughly pounded into chunky bits
» 1 cup pitted dates
» ½ tsp lemon rind
» A pinch of salt

METHOD

1. Mix the walnuts and almonds with the dates, lemon rind and a tiny pinch of salt. Knead the mixture like a dough.
2. Make a long cylindrical shape with the dough and chill in the fridge overnight.
3. Before serving, cut the cylinder into 1 cm-thick circles. Place a walnut half onto each circle as a garnish and serve.

 DATES are an excellent, nutrient-rich replacement to the empty calories of sugar. They are rich in fibre and prevent the absorption of bad cholesterol. They help to protect the colon mucus membrane. Dates are an excellent source of iron, potassium and calcium as well as B-complex vitamins and vitamin K.

- SUNSHINE PINA COLADA
- NO CREAM OF SPINACH SOUP
- PUNCHY JALAPENO HUMMUS WITH CRUDITÉS
- CHUNKY CUCUMBER IN TAHINI DRESSING
- FOXTAIL MILLET TABBOULEH
- DELIGHTFUL DOLMAS WITH PINE NUTS AND CINNAMON
- GRILLED EGGPLANT IN GARLIC AND MINT CURD
- VEGGIE-FILLED STUFFED TOMATOES
- GLUTEN-FREE PISTACHIO BAKLAVA

SUNSHINE PINA COLADA

A refreshing and filling drink that reminds us of
the beautiful sunsets by the seashore.

SERVES 2

INGREDIENTS

» 1 glass thin coconut milk, fresh (pg. 213)
» 1 glass sweet pineapple, fresh, chunks
» Ice cubes
» 2-3 tbsp raisin paste (see pg. 218), adjust to taste
» 2-3 fresh cherries for garnishing

METHOD

1. Blend together the pineapple chunks with the fresh coconut milk.
2. If not sweet enough, add some raisin paste and blend again.
3. Add ice to chill and blend again.
4. Serve garnished with cherries
5. Drink immediately and do not store this drink.

NO CREAM OF SPINACH SOUP

A nice dollop of green if you haven't had your green smoothie today.

SERVES 4-6

INGREDIENTS

» 100 gm spinach, washed thoroughly
» 1 onion, chopped
» 2 garlic cloves, chopped
» 2 cups vegetable stock (see pg. 219)
» Salt to taste
» Whipped peanut curd (see pg. 214), optional, for garnishing

METHOD

1. Steam the spinach leaves over boiling water till wilted. This takes about 5 minutes.
2. Sauté the onion and garlic, without oil, until slightly brown.
3. Blend the cooked onion, garlic and spinach together with enough stock to make a paste.
4. Transfer the blended purée into a pan with the rest of the stock.
5. Add salt to taste and cook for 5 minutes.
6. Serve hot with a swirl of peanut curd and a dash of pepper.

SPINACH like all other green vegetables is highly alkalizing and loaded with nutrients while being low in calories. It is an excellent source of iron, vitamin C and vitamin K which plays a role in strengthening bones. It is also a good source of omega-3 fatty acids.

PUNCHY JALAPENO HUMMUS WITH CRUDITÉS

There was a lovely Lebanese restaurant that we visited in London which served the best hummus. We experimented one day by adding jalapenos for our Indian palate and voila! It was an instant hit.

SERVES 4

INGREDIENTS

» 2 cups chickpeas, boiled
» 2 cloves garlic, minced
» Salt to taste
» 2-3 tbsp lime juice
» 3 tbsp tahini (see pg. 217)
» 1 whole jalapeno pepper in brine
» 5-6 whole olives

METHOD

1. Blend the chickpeas, garlic, salt, lime juice and tahini with a small amount of water, enough to move the blades and blend to a thick creamy consistency. Add more water as required.
2. Add in the jalapeno pepper and blend again.
3. Serve garnished with olives and accompanied with sticks of carrots, cucumbers, red and yellow capsicum, sliced lengthways.

If jalapenos in brine are tough to find, you can use olives, sun-dried tomatoes or simply lots of black pepper. All equally delightful!

CHUNKY CUCUMBER IN TAHINI DRESSING

Cucumbers are alkalizing, rich in fibre, water content, potassium, magnesium, vitamins and phytonutrients. They are helpful for digestive issues, diabetes, cholesterol, etc. In other words, eat more cucumbers.

SERVES 4

INGREDIENTS

» 2 large cucumbers, chopped into 2 cm cubes

For the tahini dressing:
» 2 tbsp tahini (see pg. 217)
» 2 tbsp lime juice
» 1 tbsp garlic, crushed
» ½ cup water
» Salt and pepper to taste

METHOD

1. **For the tahini dressing**, whisk together all the ingredients with a fork or blend with water. Add more water, if required.
2. Mix the tahini dressing with the cucumbers to coat evenly and serve.

This dressing can also be used with steamed vegetables like pumpkin and beans to make a healthy warm snack.

FOXTAIL MILLET TABBOULEH

Tabbouleh is a regular salad in a Mediterranean menu. We have used foxtail millet instead of bulgar wheat. It is great to reintroduce our indigenous millets into modern diets.

SERVES 4

INGREDIENTS

» 1 cup foxtail millet (Kauni or Navane), thoroughly washed, soaked in double the quantity of water for 30 minutes
» 3 cups parsley, finely chopped
» ½ cup tomatoes, diced
» ½ cup cucumber, diced
» 2 tbsp red onions, finely diced
» 2 tbsp apple cider vinegar
» Salt to taste

METHOD

1. Cook the millet by bringing the water to the boil. Then lower the heat to cook thoroughly.
2. When all the water has evaporated, turn off the heat, remove the lid and allow the mixture to dry for 10 minutes. Keep aside to cool.
3. Mix in all the ingredients with the cooled millet and serve cold.

Best place to source foxtail millet is from local farmers or organic stores. If you can't find it, you can use any small millets like kodo, proso or little millet. Some brands also sell mixed millets, which work well for this recipe.

MED
MENU
2

DELIGHTFUL DOLMAS WITH PINE NUTS AND CINNAMON

We were introduced to dolmas during our stay in London. It is hard to find the vine leaves in all countries so I have substituted it for spinach. What do you think?

SERVES 4

INGREDIENTS

» 12 large spinach leaves
» 1 cup brown rice, boiled
» 1 tsp cinnamon powder
» 1 apricot, finely chopped
» 2 tbsp pine nuts
» 2 tbsp mint, fresh, chopped
» 1 tbsp lime juice
» Salt to taste
» ½ cup vegetable stock (pg. 219)

METHOD

1. Blanch the spinach leaves in boiling hot water for 5-10 seconds keeping them as flat and open as possible.
2. Mix the rice, cinnamon powder, apricot, pine nuts, mint, lime juice and salt.
3. Separate and layout the spinach leaves individually.
4. Take 1 heaped tbsp of rice mixture and place in the bottom centre of the leaf. If the leaf is not big enough, join two or three leaves to increase the space.
5. Roll the bottom of the leaf to cover the rice. Wrap from both the sides and then roll up to form the dolma.
6. The dolmas can be served at this stage but if you prefer to have some gravy, you can follow the rest of the recipe.
7. Place the dolmas in a pan with the open end down. Pack them in tightly so they do not move or else they will open.
8. Pour ½ cup vegetable stock over the dolmas. Cover and simmer on low heat for 5-7 minutes.
9. Serve on a platter with a sprinkling of pine nuts.

GRILLED EGGPLANT IN GARLIC AND MINT CURD

This is another one of our favourites. It is simple to make, has an interesting combination of flavours, and is delicious to eat.

SERVES 4

INGREDIENTS

- » 2 medium-sized round eggplants, sliced into ½ cm-thick rounds
- » 2 cups peanut curd (see pg. 214)
- » 3 cloves garlic, crushed
- » 2 tbsp mint, finely chopped
- » Salt to taste

METHOD

1. Spread the eggplant rounds on a plate and sprinkle some salt. Let it stand for 30 minutes to allow the eggplant to release water.
2. When the eggplant is frosted with its own moisture, wipe the excess water with a paper towel or clean cloth.
3. Pre-heat the oven at 220°C for 10 minutes. Grill the eggplant slices for 15 minutes on each side.
4. Whisk the peanut curd together with garlic, mint and salt.
5. Spread the curd first on a flat serving dish.
6. Arrange the grilled eggplant around the edge of the dish.
7. Sprinkle with a few chopped mint leaves and serve.

VEGGIE FILLED STUFFED TOMATOES

This is a great recipe to use up all your leftover vegetables from the fridge. It is like eating a whole juicy tomato with delicious goodies in it!

SERVES 4

INGREDIENTS

» 4 tomatoes, cut off the tops, scoop out pulp to form empty shells
» 1 cup of diced mixed vegetables (carrots, corn kernels, peas, yellow zucchini, green zucchini, beans and onions)

For the dressing:
» 1 tbsp tahini (see pg. 217)
» 1 tbsp water
» 1 pod garlic, crushed
» 1 tbsp lime juice
» Salt to taste

METHOD

1. Steam the carrots, corn and peas for 3-5 minutes keeping them crunchy yet cooked.
2. **For the dressing**, whisk or blend the tahini with water, garlic, lime juice and salt.
3. Mix together the raw and steamed vegetables with the dressing to coat evenly.
4. Now use this vegetable mixture to fill the empty tomato shells.
5. Place the stuffed tomatoes in a pan and cover and steam for about 5 minutes, on high heat, until the tomatoes are cooked through but not soft and limp.
6. Serve hot garnished with a sprig of parsley.

If you wish to have this dish as a raw salad, then you can skip the last step of steaming the tomatoes.

GLUTEN-FREE PISTACHIO BAKLAVA

We didn't try to replace the gluten in this recipe with something else, because we felt keeping the pistachio flavour intact was more important. It's just about getting used to eating it without the greasy pastry!

SERVES 4

INGREDIENTS

- » 1 cup raw unsalted pistachio, coarsely chopped
- » ½ tsp cinnamon powder
- » ¼ cup almonds, roasted, coarsely chopped
- » 4 dried figs, finely diced
- » 2 dried apricots, finely diced
- » ½ tsp raisin paste (see pg. 218)

METHOD

1. Combine all the ingredients including the raisin paste to form a firm dough.
2. Spread the mixture on a serving plate about ½″-thick and sprinkle with pistachio flakes on top.
3. Cut into squares and chill in the fridge for minimum 3 hours.
4. Serve cold and firm.

 PISTACHIOS are rich in mono-unsaturated fatty acids like oleic acid and anti-oxidants. They help to lower LDL and increase HDL. They also have vital vitamins and minerals like iron, copper, manganese and calcium, etc. All nuts are high in fat and should be taken in moderation.

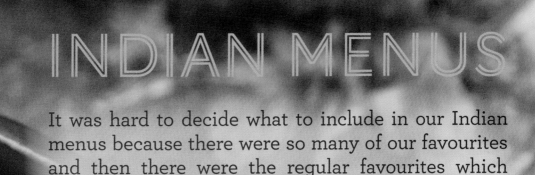

INDIAN MENUS

It was hard to decide what to include in our Indian menus because there were so many of our favourites and then there were the regular favourites which we wanted to 'veganise' and do oil-free for you. We finally decided to do a combination and keep the rest for another book! We are offering 2 grains per meal as is the norm for any special meal in India using indigenous millets which are highly nutritious and gluten free.

INDIAN MENU 1

- SPICY PAPAYA PANNA
- WINTERY TOMATO CORIANDER SOUP
- SPINACH AND ONION PAKODA WITH GREEN CHUTNEY
- CARROT, PEANUT SALAD WITH ROASTED SESAME SEEDS AND LIME DRESSING
- TEXTURED WALNUT SPINACH CURD
- SATVIK PUNJABI RAJMA
- FRAGRANT BROWN RICE
- BAJRA ROTI WITH FLAXSEED AND GINGER
- STUFFED STEAMED KARELA
- AMAZING AMARANTH ALMOND MILK KHEER

SPICY PAPAYA PANNA

One of our favourite *chatpata* drinks. We call it liquid *chaat*. It was a spontaneous creation with the participants at one of our cooking classes. It's a perfect afternoon snack when the taste buds are looking for some spicy stimulation. The chilli has a surprising and delightful bite.

SERVES 2

INGREDIENTS

- » ½ papaya
- » ½ green chilli
- » 1 tbsp lime juice
- » 1 tsp ginger, grated
- » ¼ tsp roasted cumin powder
- » Black salt to taste
- » Water and ice as required
- » *Chaat masala* to taste, optional

METHOD

1. Blend all the ingredients together till completely smooth. Add ½ glass water or more as required to achieve pouring consistency.
2. Blend with ice to get a chilled drink.
3. Garnish with a green chilli. Enjoy the zing!

WINTERY TOMATO CORIANDER SOUP

Any party hosted in Delhi's winter would serve tomato soup. It reminds us of outdoor weddings on cold nights where this warming soup would be very welcome.

SERVES 4

INGREDIENTS

» 250 gm tomatoes
» 100 gm green coriander, fresh, thick stalks separated
» 4 garlic pods, grated
» ½ green chilli, chopped, optional
» Salt to taste
» 1 tbsp date or raisin paste (see pg. 218), optional
» Black pepper to taste, optional

METHOD

1. Boil 2 cups of water with coriander stalks and garlic for 3 minutes to get a fragrant broth. Discard the coriander stalks from the boiling water and set the broth aside.
2. In a steamer, cook the tomatoes till the skin cracks. This takes about 10 minutes. Remove from heat and cool slightly.
3. Either blend and sieve the mixture or push the slightly cooled tomatoes through a sieve by crushing them with a ladle. The goal is to remove the hard parts of the skin and seeds as this can sometimes be irritating while having the soup.
4. Add this sieved liquid to the boiled garlic and coriander stalk broth. Add the green chilli, if using, and salt to taste. Bring to the boil and then simmer on low heat for 3 minutes.
5. Remove from heat and mix in the date or raisin paste and black pepper, if using.
6. Serve garnished with chopped coriander leaves.

SPINACH AND ONION PAKODA WITH GREEN CHUTNEY

It always surprises people to know that they can still have fritters (*pakodas*) despite not using oil. Baking them and changing the shape a bit is equally tasty with our all-time favourite mint chutney. Go for it! You don't have to give up *pakodas*!

SERVES 4

INGREDIENTS

For the fritters (*pakoda*):
1 cup chickpea flour
500 gm spinach leaves, chopped
2 medium-sized onions, chopped
½ tsp red chilli powder
½ tsp carom seeds
¼ tsp coriander powder
¼ tsp mango powder
Salt to taste
1 green chilli, chopped

For the green chutney:
1 cup green coriander, fresh
1 cup mint, fresh
1 green chilli
1 clove garlic
½ tsp ginger
1 tbsp tamarind paste
Salt to taste

METHOD

1. **For the fritters (*pakodas*)**, mix all the ingredients well together with your hands and squeeze the spinach to release some water for binding.
2. Place spoonfuls of this batter on a baking sheet in a baking tray, flattening them with your hand to enable thorough cooking.
3. Bake in the oven for 30 minutes at 200°C and then flip over and bake for another 10-15 minutes.
4. **For the green chutney**, blend all the ingredients together to a smooth paste. Adjust ingredients to suit your taste.
5. Serve the fritters hot accompanied with green chutney.

CARROT, PEANUT SALAD WITH ROASTED SESAME SEEDS AND LIME DRESSING

We simply love this salad because it makes raw carrots so delightful to eat and takes very little time to make.

SERVES 4-6

INGREDIENTS

- » 500 gm carrots, unpeeled, julienned into thin slivers
- » 2 tbsp raisins, soaked for 30 minutes to plump them up
- » ¼ cup peanuts, roasted, coarsely chopped
- » 2 tbsp sesame seeds, roasted
- » 2 tbsp green coriander, chopped

For the dressing:
- » 2 tbsp lime juice or ¼ cup orange juice
- » 1 tsp raisin paste (see p. 218)
- » 1 tsp cumin seeds, roasted, coarsely crushed
- » 2 cloves garlic, crushed, optional
- » Salt to taste

METHOD

1. Mix the carrots with the raisins.
2. **For the dressing**, mix all the ingredients and whisk together.
3. Add the dressing to the carrots and raisins; toss to mix thoroughly.
4. Allow the carrots to marinate in this liquid for 30 minutes to 2 hours. In hot weather, this can be done in the fridge.
5. Before serving, mix in the peanuts and half the sesame seeds and garnish with green coriander and remaining sesame seeds.

TEXTURED WALNUT SPINACH CURD

We first tasted a curd dip at a colleague's house one summer evening in Delhi and fell in love with it. Of course, we had to create a vegan version. This dish can be wonderful with crudités or a flavourful accompaniment to any Indian summer meal.

SERVES 4

INGREDIENTS

- » 2 cups soy or peanut curd (see pg. 214)
- » ½ cup spinach, steamed, cooled, chopped
- » ½ cup walnuts, chopped
- » ½ tsp garlic, grated
- » 1 tbsp raisin paste (see p. 218)
- » Salt to taste
- » 4 walnut halves, for garnishing

Photograph on pg. 149: bottom

METHOD

1. Whisk the curd until smooth.
2. Add the spinach and mix well.
3. Mix in the rest of the ingredients except the walnut halves.
4. Serve chilled garnished with the walnut halves.

WALNUTS are an excellent source of omega-3 essential fatty acids. They help lower bad cholesterol and prevent coronary artery disease when combined with a plant-based diet. They are an excellent source of vitamin E and other phytochemicals that are anti-inflammatory and protect against neurological diseases.

SATVIK PUNJABI RAJMA

For any Punjabi, *rajma chawal* is a family favourite with fond memories. This oil-free version is also *satvik* (no onion, no garlic) and will taste just as good. It might make you wonder why you are adding all the unnecessary fat to your meals.

SERVES 4

INGREDIENTS

- » 1 cup kidney beans (*rajma*), soaked overnight or for 6 hours
- » 4 cups water
- » Salt to taste
- » 4 medium-sized or 200 gm tomatoes
- » ½˝ piece ginger
- » ½ tsp cumin powder
- » ¼ tsp turmeric powder
- » 1 tsp coriander powder
- » ¼ tsp red chilli powder, optional
- » A pinch of asafoetida
- » ¼ tsp garam masala
- » 2 tbsp green coriander leaves, fresh, chopped

METHOD

1. Drain out the soaking water and wash the kidney beans thoroughly again.
2. Add salt and 4 cups water and pressure cook the beans on medium heat till the first whistle, then on low heat for a further 20 minutes.
3. In a blender, blend the tomatoes and ginger into a paste.
4. Heat a wok and when very hot, turn off the heat. Now add the cumin powder, turmeric powder, coriander powder and red chilli powder (if using) stirring constantly to dry-roast them. This will ensure that the powdered spices don't burn.
5. Turn the heat on again and to the roasted spices add the tomato-ginger paste and a little salt and cook for 10 minutes, stirring intermittently.
6. Cool 2 ladles of boiled kidney beans and purée into a paste in a blender or by mashing to thicken the gravy.
7. Now to the cooked tomato paste, add the puréed as well as the boiled kidney beans.
8. Add the asafoetida and cook without covering, on low heat, for 20 minutes.
9. Remove from heat, add the garam masala and mix well.
10. Serve garnished with green coriander leaves. Enjoy with brown rice (see pg. 150).

Photograph on pg. 149: top

FRAGRANT BROWN RICE

This rice uses what North Indians call *khada masala* or whole spices. These are very aromatic and lend an appetizing fragrance to the cooked rice.

SERVES 4

INGREDIENTS

» 1 cup dry brown rice, soaked for 2 hours, drained
» 2 large black cardamoms
» 6 whole cloves
» 1 cinnamon stick
» 2 bay leaves
» Salt to taste

Photograph on pg. 148: centre

METHOD

1. Add exactly double the amount of water in the drained rice.
2. In a medium saucepan, dry-roast the cardamom pods, cloves, cinnamon stick and bay leaves over medium heat until it emits an aroma.
3. Add the soaked rice with the fresh water and salt to the pan.
4. Cook on high heat and bring to the boil. Turn the heat to medium and simmer for 15-20 minutes until rice is tender and crushes easily when tested.

The best way to check if rice is done is to crush some grains between your fingers. Check that it is soft to the core and you don't get any grit.

BAJRA ROTI WITH FLAXSEED AND GINGER

These are delicious *rotis* or *bhakris*. A great alternative to the regular fare although it has a different making process as they don't roll as easily. Once you master the art, you will love these.

SERVES 4

INGREDIENTS

» 2 cups pearl millet (*bajra*) flour
» 1 cup lukewarm water
» 1 tsp ginger, grated
» 1 tbsp flaxseed powder
» 1 tsp green chilli paste, optional
» Salt to taste

Photograph on pg. 148: top

METHOD

1. Mix the flour with the rest of the ingredients.
2. Add warm water as needed and knead to make a soft dough.
3. Keep aside for 10-15 minutes, covered with a wet cloth.
4. Heat the griddle (*tawa*); take a handful of the kneaded dough, put it on a flat surface to flatten by patting down with your hands into a roti shape.
5. Use dry flour while shaping to avoid sticking to the surface.
6. Put the roti on the griddle and cook for a few minutes till it is easy to scrape it off from the griddle.
7. Turn and cook the other side on medium heat. Millet rotis take longer to cook so allow it to cook thoroughly.
8. Remove from heat and serve immediately.

STUFFED STEAMED KARELA

We first learnt this recipe with okra (*bhindi*) at a cooking class in Auroville. Since bitter gourd is excellent for people with diabetes, we recreated this recipe with a few adjustments. The sweetness of the coconut and added dates mellows the bitterness of the gourd and tastes delicious.

SERVES 4

INGREDIENTS

» ½ kg bitter gourd (*karela*), slit lengthways on one side to create an opening, seeds discarded if too large
» 1 cup coconut, grated
» ¼ cup chickpea flour, roasted
» 2 tsp cumin powder
» ½ tsp red chilli powder
» 1 tbsp raisin paste (see p. 218)
» 1 cup green coriander leaves, chopped
» ½ tsp turmeric powder
» ½ tsp salt
» A pinch of asafoetida
» A pinch of mango powder

METHOD

1. Mix all the ingredients (except the gourd and keep 1 tbsp grated coconut aside for garnishing) to make the stuffing (the more you stuff the better).
2. Stuff the bitter gourd with the above mixture and put in a steamer over boiling water. Steam for 10-12 minutes till the skin is soft. The skin will lose its bright green colour with cooking.
3. Serve hot garnished with the grated coconut.

This recipe works well with okra and Indian baby pumpkin (*tinda*) too.

AMAZING AMARANTH ALMOND MILK KHEER

Kheers are universally loved sweet dishes, which Indians eat at celebrations. Amaranth is a highly nutritious seed rich in calcium, iron, magnesium and essential amino acids. This recipe is quick and the *kheer* thickens as the amaranth absorbs the water.

SERVES 4-6

INGREDIENTS

» 2 glasses almond milk (see pg. 212)
» 1½ cups popped amaranth
» ¼ cup date paste (see p. 218), or more if required
» ½ tsp cinnamon powder
» 2 tbsp almonds, sliced, toasted
» A few strands saffron, optional

METHOD

1. In a pan, heat the almond milk till it comes to the first boil.
2. Mix in the amaranth, date paste and cinnamon powder; cook on medium heat for 2 minutes.
3. Remove from heat and add in saffron, if using.
4. This dessert can be served hot or cold. Chill in the refrigerator after cooling for 2-3 hours, if serving it cold.
5. Sprinkle with toasted almonds and lay out a few strands of saffron as garnish.

You can use this recipe as a hot breakfast porridge on a cold winter morning too.

INDIAN MENU 2

- FLAVOUR BLAST MASALA CHHAACH
- PUMPKIN SOUP OR KADDU SHORBA
- RED HOT BEETROOT CHOPS
- MAH PRAHAD SALAD
- CRISPY OKRA SALAD
- KADHI (SOUTH INDIAN CURD STEW WITH VEGETABLES)
- SORGHUM GARLIC ROTI / BHAKRI
- BROWN RICE PULAO WITH VEGETABLES
- CREAMY PALAK PANEER WITH TOFU
- GUILT-FREE GAJAR KA HALWA

FLAVOUR BLAST MASALA CHHAACH

This drink, a South Indian version of what Punjabis call *lassi*, is a burst of flavours. Spicy, tangy and utterly satisfying, it is quite filling so makes a great snack too.

SERVES 2

INGREDIENTS

» 1 cup peanut or soy curd (see pg. 214)
» 10-12 curry leaves
» ½ tsp ginger, grated
» Salt to taste
» ¼ green chilli
» 1 tbsp lime juice
» 1½ glass water
» ½ glass ice
» ½ tsp mustard seeds
» A pinch of asafoetida

METHOD

1. In a blender, add the curd, 4-5 curry leaves, ginger, salt and green chilli. Blend for 1 minute.
2. Now add the lime juice, water and ice and blend again till the ice is crushed.
3. Heat a pan or tempering ladle, add the remaining curry leaves and mustard seeds, sauté till the seeds start popping.
4. Remove from heat and add the asafoetida; stir well.
5. Pour the tempering over the butter milk and serve.

PUMPKIN SOUP OR KADDU SHORBA

A lovely warming thick soup, rich in vital anti-oxidants and vitamins. Use the pumpkin with the skin to get maximum fibre and nutrition.

SERVES 4

INGREDIENTS

» 250 gm pumpkin, unpeeled, chopped into cubes
» 2½ cups water
» ½ tsp fenugreek seeds
» 1-2˝ cinnamon stick
» 1-2 cloves
» ¼ tsp cumin seeds
» Salt and black pepper to taste

METHOD

1. Steam the pumpkin for 5-7 minutes till soft.
2. Grind the pumpkin with ½ cup water to a smooth consistency.
3. Boil the remaining 2 cups of water with fenugreek seeds and cinnamon stick.
4. Add in the pumpkin purée and boil for 1 minute.
5. In a dry pan, roast the cloves and cumin seeds for approximately 2 minutes till they emit a fragrance.
6. Serve hot, seasoned with salt and black pepper and garnished with roasted cloves and cumin seeds.

For a creamier taste, you can add in ½ cup of coconut milk.

RED HOT BEETROOT CHOPS

These unusual beetroot chops are a big hit in Kolkata's street food scene. Our oil-free version makes a great alternative snack and replacement for fried food cravings.

SERVES 6-8

INGREDIENTS

» 2 beetroots, grated
» 1 potato, steamed, mashed
» 4 tbsp gram flour / chickpea flour
» 1 onion, chopped
» 1 green chilli, chopped
» ½ cup black chana sprouts
» 2 tbsp green coriander leaves, chopped
» Salt to taste
» 1 tbsp flaxseed powder, optional

METHOD

1. Roast the gram flour till a fragrance is released and the raw smell disappears.
2. Sauté the onion and green chilli till soft.
3. Mix together all the ingredients.
4. Take small amounts of the mixture in the palm of your hand and form a ball. Flatten the ball and place on a griddle. Repeat till all the mixture is used up.
5. Cook the balls on medium heat till brown on both sides.
6. Serve hot with green chutney (see pg. 143) or tomato ketchup (see pg. 218).

MAH PRAHAD SALAD

This salad is inspired by the Assamese *Mah Prahad,* which is served after prayer ceremonies. We have tweaked it a bit but served it on an authentic Assamese serving dish!

SERVES 4

INGREDIENTS

- » 1 cup corn kernels, steamed
- » 1 tsp black mustard seeds
- » ¼ cup curry leaves
- » ½ cup coconut, grated
- » ½ cup moong sprouts
- » ½ cup black chana sprouts
- » ½ carrot, grated
- » 2 tbsp lime juice
- » ½ tsp ginger, finely chopped
- » 1 green chilli, finely chopped
- » 1 tbsp green coriander leaves, finely chopped
- » Salt to taste

METHOD

1. Lightly roast the mustard seeds and curry leaves in a pan. Set aside.
2. Mix the remaining ingredients together.
3. Serve seasoned with mustard seeds and curry leaves.

 ENZYMES are a type of protein that act as vital catalysts for most of our body's functions and processes. They are heat sensitive and are destroyed in the cooking process. It is estimated that sprouts may contain upto 100 times more enzymes than even raw fruits and vegetables.

CRISPY OKRA SALAD

Okra is a difficult vegetable to cook without oil, but we have successfully sourced this delicious oil-free variation. It provides the perfect crunch to your meal.

SERVES 4

INGREDIENTS

» 500 gm okra, cut into slanting pieces about 1 cm thick
» 2-3 onions, quartered, slices separated
» 2 tbsp chickpea flour
» Salt to taste
» ½ tsp red chilli powder
» 2 tomatoes, chopped
» 1 green chilli, diced, optional
» ½ cup coconut, grated

METHOD

1. Mix the flour, salt and red chilli powder together.
2. Toss the flour mixture to coat the okra and onions evenly.
3. Spread in a single layer on a non-stick baking sheet on a tray and grill for 20 minutes at 180°C.
4. Stir and change sides and grill again for 15 minutes till lightly brown and crisp. The okra will reduce quite a lot as it dehydrates and becomes crispy.
5. Remove from the oven and put into a bowl.
6. Add in the tomatoes, green chilli, if using, and sprinkle with grated coconut.
7. Mix well and serve.

Sometimes, due to the high water content of okra, it might require additional grilling time to get it crisp.

If drumsticks
are not available,
you can use lotus stem,
yam, raw banana or
any other type of
gourd.

KADHI (SOUTH INDIAN CURD STEW WITH VEGETABLES)

Kadhis are loved across India whether you go North or South. Every region has its own version. We like this South Indian version as it uses nutritious vegetables.

SERVES 4

INGREDIENTS

» 1 cup peanut curd (see pg. 214)
» 1 heaped tbsp chickpea flour
» 4 cups water
» ¼ tsp turmeric powder
» ½ tsp salt or to taste
» 1 long drumstick, cut into 3″ pieces
» ½ tsp dry mango powder
» 2 cups pumpkin or bottle gourd with skin, chopped
» ½ coconut, grated
» 1-2 green chillies
» 1 tsp black pepper powder, optional

For the tempering:
» 1-2 dried red chillies
» ½ tsp mustard seeds
» ¼ tsp cumin seeds, optional
» A few curry leaves

METHOD

1. Roast the chickpea flour in a pan, on medium heat, stirring constantly, till it emits an aroma. This should take 3-4 minutes. Set aside to cool.
2. In a pan, add 1 cup water, turmeric powder and ½ tsp salt with the drumstick and bring to the boil. Cover and simmer on medium heat for 4-5 minutes till half done.
3. Whisk together the curd, chickpea flour and dry mango powder with 3 cups water till smooth. The consistency should not be too thick as it would thicken further with cooking.
4. Add the curd mixture and pumpkin to the boiled drumstick and bring to the boil on low heat, stirring constantly. Keep uncovered so it does not boil over. Cook on low heat as the curd can separate on high heat. This may take 10 minutes.
5. In a grinder, make a paste of the fresh coconut, green chilli, remaining salt and black pepper (if using) adding a little water.
6. Add the coconut paste to the *kadhi* and stir to mix well. Bring to the boil on low heat and simmer for 2-3 minutes.
7. Test that the vegetables are soft and adjust the salt. Remove from heat and keep covered.
8. **For the tempering**, in a small pan, dry-roast the red chillies and mustard seeds for 1 minute before adding the cumin seeds (if using) and curry leaves. When the mustard seeds start to pop remove from heat.
9. Sprinkle over the *kadhi* to finish. Garnish with a red chilli. Serve hot with rice and a crispy poppadom (*papad*).

SORGHUM GARLIC ROTI / BHAKRI

An age-old recipe that brings back millets into our diet.

SERVES 4

INGREDIENTS

» 2 cups sorghum flour
» Salt to taste
» 2 tsp freshly cracked black pepper
» 1 tsp garlic paste
» ¼ cup green coriander leaves, finely chopped
» 1 cup lukewarm water

METHOD

1. Mix the sorghum flour with salt, black pepper, garlic paste and green coriander.
2. Add warm water, as needed, and knead to make a soft dough. Keep aside for 15-20 minutes, covered with a wet cloth.
3. Divide the dough equally into small portions.
4. Heat the griddle (*tawa*); shape each portion into a ball and put on a wet cloth. Pat to flatten and shape into a roti.
5. Pick the whole cloth to transfer the roti to the hot griddle (as shown).
6. Spread a tablespoon of water on the roti to moisten it, like you would use oil.
7. Cook for a few minutes till it is easy to scrape off the roti from the griddle. Turn and cook till brown. Millet rotis take longer to cook so be patient.
8. Remove from heat and serve immediately.

For variation, you can use 1 cup fresh dill and ginger paste. Don't store the rotis for later use as they soak up all the water and become hard.

BROWN RICE PULAO WITH VEGETABLES

Is no oil pulao possible? Yes, it absolutely is! This brown rice dish ensures that all the fibre and vitamins remain intact.

SERVES 4

INGREDIENTS

- » 1 cup brown rice
- » 2 cups mixed vegetables (any combination of cauliflower, carrots, peas, green beans), chopped
- » 1 onion, sliced
- » 1″ cinnamon stick
- » 4 cloves
- » 1 big black cardamom
- » 1-2 bay leaves
- » Salt to taste

METHOD

1. Soak the rice for 2 hours in double the amount of water. Change the water keeping the amount double.
2. Mix ½ tsp salt with the onion and keep aside to sweat.
3. In a pan, bring the rice and water to the boil. Lower heat and simmer for 10 minutes.
4. Without oil, sauté the onion till brown; keep aside for garnishing.
5. Without oil, sauté the vegetables and spices and cook, on low heat, for 4-5 minutes by sprinkling some dashes of water to allow the flavours to infuse with each other. The vegetables should be half cooked.
6. Add the half-cooked vegetables to the rice and mix well with salt. Cook, covered, for another 10 minutes on low heat.
7. When the rice is fully cooked and before the vegetables disintegrate, remove from heat.
8. Serve hot garnished with browned onions.

Salting the onions and keeping them for 10 minutes allows them to sweat. This ensures that they don't stick to the pan when cooked. This is our special 'dry-fry' method for browning onions.

CREAMY PALAK PANEER WITH TOFU

No trip to India by a visitor is complete without having our delicious *palak paneer*. Originally from the North, this dish is well adapted in all parts of India now. No self-respecting North Indian restaurant in the world will skip having this on their menu. Enjoy this healthy version.

SERVES 4

INGREDIENTS

- » 500 gm spinach
- » 150-200 gm tofu (soy *paneer*), cut into 1˝ cubes
- » 2 tbsp savoury cashew cream (see pg. 215)
- » 2 tsp cumin powder
- » 2 onions, thinly sliced
- » 1 onion, roughly chopped
- » 1˝ piece ginger
- » 2 cloves garlic
- » Salt to taste
- » 1 tsp red chilli powder

METHOD

1. Marinate the tofu with cashew cream, salt and cumin powder for half an hour.
2. Blanch the spinach in boiling water till just wilted; set aside to cool.
3. Meanwhile in a wok, sauté the thinly sliced onions till transparent on medium heat.
4. Grind the other onion, ginger and the garlic cloves to a fine paste. Add this paste to the sautéed onions and cook for 3-4 minutes on medium heat.
5. Purée the spinach leaves in a blender and add the purée and the chilli powder to the wok. Add some water, if necessary, so it is not too dry. Let it boil for a minute or two.
6. Add the tofu to the spinach, lower heat and simmer for 5 more minutes.
7. Serve hot with a drizzle of savoury cashew cream.

GUILT FREE GAJAR KA HALWA

Delhi winter memories are sweetened with thoughts of hot *gajar halwa*. The regular version has sugar, ghee, whole milk fudge (*khoya*) and milk and takes hours to prepare. When we first made this in a few minutes for a friend, she could not believe how good it tasted and how light she felt afterwards.

SERVES 4

INGREDIENTS

- » 3 large red carrots, grated
- » 1 tbsp raisins
- » ¾ cup sweet raisin paste (see pg. 218)
- » 2 tbsp sweet cashew cream (see pg. 215)
- » ¼ tbsp cardamom powder
- » 4 tbsp almonds, toasted or raw

METHOD

1. Cook the carrots on medium heat in a covered wok. Allow it to cook in its own juices for 10-15 minutes, stirring occasionally.
2. Add the whole raisins, sweet raisin paste, cashew cream and cardamom powder; cook for another 2-3 minutes to mix in thoroughly.
3. Serve hot garnished with almonds.

Ensure that the raisins are not sour, otherwise it will make your dessert sour. You could also use date paste except that it makes the dish darker than it should be.

AMERICAN MENUS

The emerging Californian cuisine has a refreshing character of its own emphasizing beautiful presentation and fresh local ingredients. We tried to mix some of our all-time favourites with some new fusion recipes that have come to represent American food in this part of the world.

- DECADENT KEY LIME SMOOTHIE
- NUTRITIOUS BROCCOLI SOUP
- JACKET POTATO BOATS
- ZUCCHINI PARCELS WITH BEET, CARROT AND CHIA DRESSING
- ALTERNATIVE CAESAR'S SALAD
- UNBELIEVABLE VEGAN PIZZA
- HEARTY LENTIL LOAF
- BEETROOT RAVIOLI WITH WALNUT CREAM IN APPLE CIDER SAUCE
- FRUITY BANANA SPLIT WITH ICE-CREAM

DECADENT KEY LIME SMOOTHIE

For all those who love the tart flavours of key lime pie, this smoothie indulges the taste-buds without compromising on health.

SERVES 2

INGREDIENTS

» 1 whole small lime, peeled, quartered
» ¼ cup cashews, raw, soaked for 1 hour
» ½ cup raisins, soaked
» 1 medium-sized banana, fresh or frozen
» 5 tbsp lemon juice, freshly squeezed
» 1 tsp vanilla extract
» ½ tsp lemon zest, freshly grated
» A pinch of Himalayan rock salt
» 2 cups ice

METHOD

1. Blend the cashews with a little water to form a paste.
2. Remove any hard flesh and pips of the peeled and quartered lime and put in the blender
3. Add in the raisins with the soaking water and blend till completely smooth.
4. Now add in all the remaining ingredients and the cashew paste; blend till smooth.
5. Serve chilled. Delicious, it's like a liquid dessert!

NUTRITIOUS BROCCOLI SOUP

A soup for the soul! It is creamy, warming and delicious.
You wouldn't believe that this soup has no
cream, milk or butter!

SERVES 4

INGREDIENTS

» 1 small broccoli, chopped
» 1 onion, chopped
» 2 cups vegetable stock (see pg. 219)
» Salt and pepper to taste

METHOD

1. Sauté the onions without oil until transparent.
2. Add the broccoli and 4 tbsp stock and steam for
   4-5 minutes.
3. Transfer to a blender and blend to a smooth, creamy
   consistency by adding the remaining stock.
4. The thickness of the soup can be adjusted according to
   your taste by adding or reducing the stock amount.
5. Remove from the blender and heat in a pan. Add salt
   and pepper to taste and serve.

JACKET POTATO BOATS

Everybody loves potatoes and the best way to eat them is without oil and with the skin on. Some of the best nutrition that it has to offer, is right under the skin of the potato. Try this out!

SERVES 4

INGREDIENTS

» 2 large potatoes
» ¼ cup almond milk
» ½ cup mixed vegetables (peas, corn kernels, diced carrots and broccoli)
» Salt and black pepper to taste
» ½ tsp mustard sauce

METHOD

1. Steam the potatoes for 10 minutes so that they are parboiled and easy to bake.
2. Bake the parboiled potatoes with the skin, in the oven, at 220·C, for 20 minutes. Flip the potatoes over and bake for another 15 minutes till the skin is stiff and dry.
3. Remove from the oven, cool slightly and halve them lengthways.
4. Scoop the potato out from both the halves leaving an empty shell.
5. Mash the scooped out potato with the almond milk to make a creamy consistency. Add the vegetables, salt, pepper and mustard sauce; mix well.
6. Scoop spoonfuls of this mixture back into the jacket halves.
7. Sprinkle black pepper and grill for 5 minutes on high heat until brown.
8. Serve hot.

It's a love / hate relationship with the POTATO and there is a lot of misunderstanding around it. These tubers are one of the richest sources of B-complex vitamins and also contain many essential minerals, fibre and other nutrients. Eat potatoes with the skin on after washing it thoroughly.

AMERICAN
MENU
1

ZUCCHINI PARCELS WITH BEET, CARROT AND CHIA DRESSING

SERVES 4

INGREDIENTS

» 1 medium-sized zucchini
» 1 carrot, julienned
» ½ beetroot, julienned
» 3 tbsp lime juice
» 1 tbsp ginger juice
» Salt to taste
» 1 tsp chia seeds

METHOD

1. Peel the zucchini with a wide peeler to create thin strips and fold to make circular loops.
2. Place these on a serving plate and fill with the carrot and beetroot. Squeeze ½ tsp lime juice and sprinkle some salt over the vegetables.
3. Mix the rest of the lime juice and ginger juice along with salt. Soak the chia seeds in this for 10 minutes. Add a little water if they drink up all the juice.
4. Drizzle the dressing over the salad just before serving.

Popular for their high vitamin C content and highly alkalizing, LIMES AND LEMONS have many other beneficial health properties. They contain various phytochemicals, which serve as antioxidants, free radical scavengers with anti-inflammatory properties, and modulate the immune system. They are also rich in essential minerals which are alkalizing for the body.

ALTERNATIVE CAESAR'S SALAD

Hmm! Did you give up on Caesar's salad? Don't! Here is how to have it with vegan mayonnaise and no croutons...

SERVES 4

INGREDIENTS

» 1 head of romaine lettuce (or any other), washed, dried, torn with hands
» ½ cup walnut halves
» 1 cup cashew mayonnaise (see pg. 216)

METHOD

1. Mix the walnut halves with the lettuce.
2. Serve the salad and dressing separately to avoid wilting of lettuce leaves.
3. The cashew mayonnaise dressing can be folded in just before eating.

If you really want to have crunchy croutons, then you can break some oats crackers (pg. 29) into the salad.

UNBELIEVABLE VEGAN PIZZA

This is unfailingly the most popular recipe in all the wellness retreats we have done. It is by far the number one choice for all. Check your fridge for leftover veggies as anything will taste good!

SERVES 4

INGREDIENTS

For the gluten-free base:
» 2 cups sorghum flour
» ½ cup coconut milk (see pg. 213)
» Salt to taste

For the topping:
» 2 cups milanese tomato sauce (see pg. 219)
» 1 cup broccoli florets, blanched

» 1 onion ring, sliced
» ½ cup mushroom, sliced
» ½ cup yellow pepper, sliced
» 1 cup cashew herb cheese (see pg. 216)
» 2 tbsp roasted garlic (see pg. 70)
» 1 tsp dry red chillies, crushed
» 1 tsp dried oregano
» A few drops Tabasco sauce
» A handful basil leaves, fresh, for garnishing
» 2 tbsp olives, sliced for garnishing

METHOD

1. **For the gluten-free base**, knead the sorghum flour, coconut milk and salt together.
2. Spread the dough with your fingers to form a round shape. The dough will not roll out and we are not going to bake it. This dough will only give us small circles and it will split if we try to make them too big. Use a wet kitchen towel to help you spread the circle, if necessary.
3. Place on a flat pan and cook on both sides until slightly brown and fully cooked. Set aside.
4. Spread the milanese tomato sauce generously on the pizza base. The base tends to be a bit dry if the sauce is scanty.
5. Lay all the fresh vegetables on top of the tomato sauce decoratively and distribute the colours of the vegetables evenly.
6. Top with spoonfuls of tomato sauce and cashew cheese.
7. Sprinkle with roasted garlic, chilli flakes, oregano and hot Tabasco sauce.
8. Cook under the grill for 5 minutes until the cashew cheese is slightly brown.
9. Serve hot garnished with fresh basil leaves and sliced black olives.

You can make the dough softer by adding ¼ tsp yeast while kneading. Allow the dough to stand for 3 hours before rolling.

HEARTY LENTIL LOAF

Our fridge is never void of this loaf.
You can have it as a snack or a meal with
some salad, hot or cold, fresh or two
days old. We personally think
it gets tastier as it matures.

SERVES 6

INGREDIENTS

- » ½ cup washed red lentils (*dhuli masoor*)
- » ½ cup whole red lentils (*masoor*), soaked for 30 minutes, drained
- » 1 cup flaked oats
- » 1 cup mixed vegetables (carrots, beans, red capsicum), finely diced
- » 1 onion, finely diced
- » 1 tsp oregano
- » ¼ tsp roasted cumin powder
- » 2 tbsp mixed seeds (watermelon, sunflower, cucumber, flaxseed, etc.)
- » 6 tbsp homemade tomato ketchup (see pg. 218)
- » Salt to taste

METHOD

1. In a saucepan, add 2 cups fresh water along with the soaked lentils and the washed red lentils. Boil for 20 minutes on medium heat till it is cooked but not mashed. It should retain its shape.
2. Allow to cool for some time, then mix in all the ingredients. Make sure the mixture is a little moist or else it will be too dry after baking.
3. Place the mixture in a loaf baking tin.
4. Cover it with a layer of tomato ketchup and bake at 180 °C for 1 hour.
5. Serve hot or cold. If left overnight in the fridge, it is easier to cut like a cake.

BEETROOT RAVIOLI WITH WALNUT CREAM IN APPLE CIDER SAUCE

This is the magic of Californian fusion. An Italian pasta made with a vegetable and no oil. Looks amazing and tastes light and nutty.

SERVES 4

INGREDIENTS

» 2 large beetroots
» ½ cup cashew herb cheese (see pg. 216)
» ½ cup walnuts, roughly chopped

For the dressing:
» 4 tbsp apple cider vinegar
» 2 tbsp apple juice
» 1 tsp greens of spring onions, chopped
» 1 tsp walnuts, crushed
» Salt to taste

METHOD

1. Pressure-cook the beetroots for 10-15 minutes or till 2 whistles until it is cooked but firm. Set aside to cool.
2. Cut the beetroots into thin slices with a sharp knife. (Here we have used a special cutter to get the edges like ravioli but that's not necessary. You may cut them in rounds.)
3. Place half of the beetroot slices on a plate.
4. Combine the cashew cheese with the chopped walnuts to make a thicker consistency.
5. Drop some of this herb cheese at the centre of each beetroot slice.
6. Cover the cheese with another slice of beetroot pressing the sides lightly.
7. **For the dressing**, mix together all the ingredients mentioned. Store in the fridge until ready to serve.
8. Just before serving arrange the ravioli neatly on a plate and drizzle with the dressing. This has to be done immediately before serving or the beetroot will bleed too much colour.

FRUITY BANANA SPLIT WITH ICE-CREAM

We had great fun inventing this healthy version of a favourite from our teen years. As lovers of vegan ice-cream, this is a perfect treat even for adults. You will not believe how good the chocolate sauce can taste without any sugar or milk fat. Now you can have as much as you like and never feel heavy.

INGREDIENTS

For the chocolate ice cream:
» 2 ripe bananas
» ½ cup almond butter (see pg. 216)
» 2 tbsp cocoa powder
» 4 tbsp date paste (see pg. 218)
» ¼ tsp vanilla powder

For the mango ice cream:
» 1 ripe mango, peeled, roughly chopped

For the chocolate sauce:
» 2 tbsp date paste (see pg. 218)
» 1 tbsp cocoa powder
» 2 tbsp almond milk (see pg. 212)

For the garnish:
» 1 tbsp mix of dried raisins / cranberries / blackcurrants / blueberries
» 1 ripe but firm banana

METHOD

1. For the chocolate ice cream, blend 2 of the ripest bananas to get a smooth consistency.
2. Add the almond butter, cocoa powder and date paste; blend till smooth
3. Pour this mixture into a container for freezing.
4. When half frozen in about 6 hours, take out the container and stir the ice-cream well.
5. Seal and put back in the freezer for another 4 hours till the ice-cream is ready.
6. For the mango ice cream, blend the mango to a smooth consistency; freeze.
7. After 4 hours, stir to remove crystals and freeze again.
8. For the chocolate sauce, mix the date paste with the cocoa powder to make chocolate sauce. To get a pouring/consistency, add the almond milk and mix again.
9. To assemble, peel and slice one ripe but firm banana into half lengthways.
10. Add 3 scoops of ice-cream in the middle of the two banana halves.Pour the chocolate sauce over.
11. Top with your choice of dried berries or raisins. Enjoy the healthy deliciousness of this raw treat!

- BASIC GREEN SMOOTHIE
- NO CREAM OF MUSHROOM SOUP
- GREEN PEA PESTO WITH MILLET NACHOS
- CORN AND AVOCADO SALAD 'TO GO'
- COLESLAW WITH VEGAN MAYO
- BAKED FALAFEL BURGER
- POTATO COUNTRY 'FRIES'
- BROWN RICE CALIFORNIA SUSHI ROLLS
- BLACKCURRANT CHEESECAKE IN CINNAMON GRANOLA

BASIC GREEN SMOOTHIE

This delightful nutrient rich, dense, green drink is truly a remarkable discovery. It combines the goodness of raw green leaves with fresh fruit. It is almost synonymous with healthy eating and tastes much better than it looks! Beware, you can get addicted to it.

SERVES 2

INGREDIENTS

» 2 cups leafy greens (spinach, beet greens, pok choy, etc.)
» 1 cup water
» 1 ripe banana
» 1 tsp lime juice or ¼ tsp grated ginger
» Ice, if you like it chilled, optional

METHOD

1. Add the water to the greens and blend till completely liquidized.
2. Add in the remaining ingredients and blend some more to achieve a thick shake-like consistency.
3. Serve chilled!

It is recommended that you rotate the fresh greens of the season with any pulpy seasonal fruits like papaya, mango, grapes, etc.

NO CREAM OF MUSHROOM SOUP

We call this 'no cream of mushroom soup'. Although it looks creamy, it is totally fat free.

SERVES 4

INGREDIENTS

» 250 gm mushrooms, roughly chopped
» 1 medium-sized onion, chopped
» 2 cups vegetable stock (see pg. 219)
» Salt and pepper to taste
» 2 tbsp spring onions or chives, chopped for garnishing

METHOD

1. Dry-fry the onion until transparent.
2. Add the mushrooms and sauté until the water is released.
3. Remove and transfer into a blender. Blend into a smooth, creamy consistency by adding vegetable stock.
4. The thickness of the soup can be adjusted according to your taste by adding more or less vegetable stock as required.
5. Remove from the blender, transfer to a pan and heat through. Season to taste.
6. Serve hot, garnished with spring onions or chives.

If you prefer a clear soup, then just finely dice the mushrooms and skip the blending step. For a creamier version, add in half a cup of almond milk.

GREEN PEA PESTO WITH MILLET NACHOS

Healthy nachos? Yes, we neither use corn to make it, nor do we smother it in cheese sauce. But who says nachos can't be made of millets and covered with a low fat green pesto?

SERVES 4

INGREDIENTS

For the pesto:
» 1 cup shelled peas
» 1 onion, sliced
» Salt and black pepper to taste

For the millet crackers:
» 1 cup finger millet flour (or any other gluten-free flour)
» 1 tbsp peanut butter (see pg. 217)
» 1 tbsp coconut, fresh, grated or desiccated coconut
» ½-1 cup water
» Salt to taste
» 1 tbsp white sesame seeds

METHOD

1. **For the pesto,** sauté the peas and onion, on medium heat, for 2-3 minutes in a pan until the peas release their fragrance. Remove from heat and set aside to cool.
2. Mix in the salt and pepper.
3. Add 2 tbsp water and blend to make a smooth paste.
4. **For the millet crackers,** mix all the ingredients together except sesame seeds to form a paste.
5. Spread the paste with your fingers to form a thin layer on a non-stick baking sheet spread on the baking tray. Sprinkle the sesame seeds evenly on top.
6. Bake at 180 °C for 15 minutes. Pull out the tray and make the markings for breaking the crackers later. Bake again for 30 minutes at 180 °C till crisp.
7. Cool and break along the marked lines.
8. Use the pesto as a dip or spread the pesto sauce over the crackers just before serving.

You can also make mushroom pesto by replacing the peas with mushrooms in this recipe.

CORN AND AVOCADO SALAD 'TO GO'

This is a clever idea for carrying salad to work or anywhere else. Usually, dressings tend to make the salads soggy after a while. Here, you put the dressing at the bottom and pile up your salads on top. Then you simply upturn your jar just before eating to mix in the dressing and enjoy a fresh tasting salad.

SERVES 4

INGREDIENTS

» 2 cups sweet corn kernels
» 1 large ripe avocado, chopped
» 1 juice of lime
» Salt and black pepper to taste
» 2 tbsp black olives, sliced
» 1 cup regular or cherry tomatoes, chopped
» 1 lime, sliced, optional

METHOD

1. In a glass mason jar, squeeze the lime and dust the bottom with a little salt and pepper.
2. Next add the corn to form the bottom layer, followed by the avocado and olives.
3. Top with tomatoes and the lime slices (optional) and close the lid.
4. Refrigerate, in hot weather, till ready to eat.
5. Before eating, upturn the salad jar and give it a shake to allow the lime dressing at the bottom to mix with the salad.
6. If you want freshly squeezed lime then you can do that just before eating.
7. Dig in with your fork and enjoy!

You can layer any salad vegetables and greens of the season with a runny dressing at the bottom and take it with you 'to go'!

COLESLAW WITH VEGAN MAYO

A great accompaniment to burgers and even a delicious sandwich spread. Make it and see if anyone can spot the difference between the oily mayonnaise and our healthier version.

SERVES 4

INGREDIENTS

» 1 carrot, julienned into matchstick sizes
» ¼ medium-sized cabbage, thinly shredded
» ½ onion, thinly sliced lengthwise
» 3 tbsp cashew mayonnaise (see pg. 216)
» Salt to taste

METHOD

1. Mix the cashew mayonnaise with the carrot, cabbage and onion; toss well.
2. Adjust salt as required.

BAKED FALAFEL BURGER

We debated whether to put this recipe in the Mediterranean section, as falafels are the popular street foods from Egypt, Turkey, etc. However, their use as a burger patty makes them part of the nouvelle cuisine of California.

SERVES 4

INGREDIENTS

» 1½ cups chickpeas, cooked
» 1 medium-sized onion, finely diced
» 2 cloves garlic, minced
» 2 medium-sized carrots, grated
» 2 celery stalks, strings removed and thinly diced
» ½ cup oat flakes
» 2 tsp mixed herbs
» 1 tbsp flaxseed powder
» 1 tsp cumin powder
» 1 tbsp lime juice
» 2 tbsp tahini or sesame butter (see pg. 217)
» ¼ cup parsley or green coriander leaves, fresh
» Salt to taste
» Freshly ground black pepper to taste
» 1 tsp red chilli powder, optional
» 2 tbsp coconut milk, optional

METHOD

1. Preheat the oven to 200 °C. Line the tray with silicone mat or butter paper so that it does not stick.
2. Add some salt to the onion to allow it to sweat. Then sauté in a wok till transparent.
3. Now add the garlic and carrots and sauté for 3 minutes till the carrots are wilted and garlic is golden. Set aside to cool slightly.
4. In a food processor, add the drained chickpeas with the remaining ingredients.
5. Also add the sautéed mixture and pulse together till coarsely ground but not puréed.
6. Scoop out the mixture and roll into falafel-like oval and slightly flattened balls.
7. Bake for 20 minutes. Flip over gently and bake another 10 minutes.
8. Brush with coconut milk to prevent drying, if required.
9. To make a falafel burger you can serve this in gluten-free pita pocket or buns.
10. Add a layer of coleslaw and some shredded lettuce or sliced tomatoes and cucumber as per your preference.
11. Serve hot with coleslaw (see pg. 205) and 'fries' (see pg. 207).

Photograph on pg. 204: centre

POTATO COUNTRY 'FRIES'

Quintessentially American, I recall enjoying the fried version at many an American diner on our road trips. The little bit of natural fat from coconut, brushed on the potatoes in this baked version, does the trick and makes these 'fries' equally indulgent.

SERVES 4

INGREDIENTS

» 4 large potatoes
» ½ cup thick coconut milk (see pg. 213)
» 1 tsp mixed herbs
» Salt and black pepper to taste

METHOD

1. Steam the potatoes for 10-15 minutes to partially cook them. Larger sized potatoes will require more time. You can cut those into half to make it quicker.
2. Cool slightly and slice into thick wedges.
3. Whisk together the coconut milk, herbs and salt and pepper.
4. Coat the potatoes by brushing with coconut milk dressing. Set aside to marinate for 20 minutes.
5. Bake at 200 °C hot oven for 25 minutes on one side. Change sides and bake for another 15 minutes. Serve hot.

Photograph on pg. 204: extreme right

BROWN RICE CALIFORNIA SUSHI ROLLS

The advantage of brown rice sushi is that the fibre present provides a feeling of fullness while still being light on the stomach. The seaweed nori is an excellent source of minerals. Eat this as part of a meal or as a stand-alone snack. It's delicious!.

SERVES:

INGREDIENTS

- » 2 nori sheets
- » ¼ cup brown rice to yield 1 cup cooked brown rice, soaked for 2 hours, drained, washed
- » 1 tsp rice vinegar
- » ¼ tsp raisin paste (see pg. 218)
- » ½ avocado, cut into thin strips
- » ½ cucumber, cut into thin strips
- » 1 tomato, sliced
- » ½ yellow capsicum or carrot, cut into thin strips
- » 3 tbsp cashew mayonnaise (see pg. 216)
- » Salt to taste
- » 1 tbsp toasted sesame seeds
- » 1 tsp wasabi paste
- » ½ cup soy sauce
- » a few pieces Japanese pickled ginger

METHOD

1. Add 3 times the amount of water and 1 tsp salt to the rice and bring to the boil, on medium heat, for 15-20 minutes till all the water is absorbed.
2. Stir vigorously 3-4 times to make the rice sticky. Don't mash completely. It should be partly broken. Allow the rice to cool.
3. Mix the vinegar and raisin paste into the rice making sure the rice is sticky and not a pulp.
4. On a sushi rolling mat, lay out the nori sheet. Spread a thin layer of rice on it evenly with your fingers making sure you leave 1 cm of nori sheet free for sealing.
5. Place the strips of vegetables on the rice and spoon the cashew mayonnaise over the vegetables.
6. With the help of the sushi mat, roll the nori very tightly to form a cylindrical shape.
7. Once the roll is formed, sprinkle toasted sesame seeds over the entire roll.
8. Use a clean sharp serrated knife to cut into 1″ cylinders. Keep cleaning the knife as you cut the slices in order to keep the sticky rice away from touching the nori of the next slice.
9. Serve with wasabi, soy sauce and Japanese ginger.

BLACKCURRANT CHEESECAKE IN CINNAMON GRANOLA

This cheesecake is out of this world. No one believes that there is no sugar or cheese in the recipe. Try it and you will be remembered for it.

SERVES 4

INGREDIENTS

For the granola base:
- » 1 cup walnuts, roughly chopped
- » ½ cup almonds, roughly chopped
- » 2 dried figs, finely chopped
- » ¼ cup raisins
- » 1 cup pitted dates, chopped
- » 1 cup rolled oat flakes
- » 1 tsp cinnamon powder

For the filling:
- » 2 cups sweet cashew cream (see pg. 215)
- » 2 tbsp raisin paste (see pg. 218)
- » 1 tsp orange rind (peel), grated

For the topping:
- » 1 cup blackcurrants, soaked
- » ½ tsp orange rind
- » 2 tbsp pomegranate seeds

METHOD

1. **For the granola base,** combine all the ingredients and bake in the oven at 160 °C for 20 minutes until crisp. Set to cool.
2. **For the filling,** mix the raisin paste with the cashew cream and add the orange rind. Fold all together to make the filling.
3. Because this cheesecake does not hold together very well, it can be served in individual serving bowls or glasses.
4. Layer a serving glass with the granola and the cashew cream.
5. **For the topping,** grind the blackcurrants to a thick jam-like consistency.
6. Pour evenly on top according to taste. If you like your dessert sweet, go for it. Decorate with orange rind and pomegranate seeds
7. Refrigerate and chill for at least ½ an hour before eating.

If fresh blueberries are available, you can use a blueberry pulp instead of blackcurrants. You may need to increase the white raisins in the cream filling for more sweetness.

BASIC RECIPES

DAIRY REPLACEMENT RECIPES

OIL AND SUGAR REPLACEMENT AND FREQUENTLY USED RECIPES

ALMOND MILK

A delicious alternative to cow's milk, almonds are rich in calcium and vitamin E.

INGREDIENTS
½ cup almonds, soaked overnight or for 6 hrs minimum; 200 ml water

METHOD
1. Blend the almonds with 50 ml water and grind to a smooth paste.
2. Pour in the remaining water. You can adjust the desired thickness by using less or more water. Blend again thoroughly.
3. Pour the mixture through a muslin cloth to get smooth almond milk.

YIELD – 300 ML MILK

USAGE
1. This milk can be had cold or hot and used for hot porridges or desserts to replace milk.
2. It can be stored in the fridge for up to 3 days. Shake well before using.
3. Reserve the almond pulp as it can be added to muesli, sauces or curries.
4. To sweeten, you can add a pitted date while blending.

For use in muesli or cereals, there is no need to strain the milk. Enjoy the crunchiness of the almonds.

SOY MILK

It is good to make this at home, to avoid pesticides and GMO soy. It requires a little more work than almond milk.

INGREDIENTS:
100 gm organic soy beans, washed, soaked in water overnight; 1 litre water

METHOD
1. Wash the soaked soy beans in the morning thoroughly and remove the skin while washing.
2. In a blender, blend the soy beans first with a little water to make a smooth paste.
3. Then add the remaining water and blend till smooth.
4. Strain the milk out through a mesh cloth to get soy milk.
4. Put the soy milk in a vessel and bring to the boil, on medium heat, while stirring it at regular intervals.
6. When boiled, lower the heat and simmer for another 8-10 minutes so that soy beans are thoroughly cooked.
7. Let it cool down to room temperature and refrigerate.

YIELD -1 LITRE

USAGE
· Soy milk is great for replacing milk in recipes.
· Makes great milk shakes and yoghurt.
· It can be stored in the fridge for up to 5 days.

PEANUT MILK

INGREDIENTS
100 gm raw peanuts, washed, soaked for 2 hrs; 1 litre water

METHOD
1. Drain the peanuts and rinse.
2. Blend the peanuts in a blender till you get a smooth paste, adding a little water if required.
3. Then add the remaining water to the paste and blend again to make the milk.
4. If you like smoother milk, strain the mixture through a muslin cloth and discard the fibre. I usually keep the fibre as it makes thicker curd. If you want thicker milk without fibre, you can double the peanuts to 200 gm or reduce the water to 500 ml.
5. Pour it into a pan and bring to the boil. Reduce the heat and bring to the boil at least 2-3 times so that the peanuts are well cooked. This would take 4-5 minutes.

YIELD – 1 LITRE MILK

USAGE
• Peanut milk works well to make peanut curd, which is good for buttermilk and curd rice and even *raitas*, but not so great to drink as milk.
• Use fresh, don't store as milk.

COCONUT MILK

INGREDIENTS
1 cup mature coconut, fresh, grated tightly packed (not the green, tender, drinking coconut); 200 ml hot, but not boiling water; 100 ml normal temperature water for thin milk

METHOD
1. In a pan, add the grated coconut and pour the hot water over it. Allow it to sit for 10 minutes.
2. Once lukewarm, blend thoroughly by adding half the water. Then add the remaining water and blend again.
3. Sieve this through a muslin cloth and discard the fibre. This will yield thick milk.
4. If you want thin milk, add the remaining normal temperature water.
5. Optional - You could also do a second extraction by blending the discarded fibre again with 100 ml warm water and it would yield thin milk.

YIELD – 150 ML THICK MILK OR 250 ML THIN MILK

USAGE
• This milk can be used to replace milk in any recipe. Great for curries (thin milk) and ice-creams (thick milk) due to the fat content of coconut.
• Preferably use this fresh. It can be stored in the fridge for up to 2 days but will separate, so just give it a shake before using.

If, in a hurry, you could just blend the grated coconut with warm water and sieve. However, the hot water method above ensures better extraction.

Peanut curd

SOY OR PEANUT CURD

INGREDIENTS:
1 litre soy milk or 1 litre peanut milk (with or without fibre); 2 tbsp vegan curd starter or 10 green chillies

METHOD
1. In a pan, bring the milk to the boil. Lower the heat and cook for another 6-8 minutes. If using unstrained peanut milk, just stir the milk, occasionally, to prevent burning from the bottom. Soy milk needs to be boiled and cooked for 10 minutes.
2. Allow the milk to cool to lukewarm or body temperature.
3. Use 2 tbsp of vegan curd as starter. Whisk it thoroughly, adding a little milk to smoothen. Mix this in to the milk to be set as curd. Ensure that the starter is mixed thoroughly and evenly.
4. Allow the milk vessel to rest in a warm, undisturbed place with no air draft, for 8 hours or overnight till you get thick curd. In the old days, the pan was wrapped with a light blanket to provide warmth, especially in winters.
5. If you don't have a vegan starter, borrow from a vegan friend or use regular dairy curd starter to begin with.

ALTERNATIVE METHOD
1. If you don't want to use dairy milk curd as a starter (and we appreciate that), use the green chillies' method. Yes, you read that right! Break off the top of 10 green chillies with your hand and add only the tops with the stems attached to the milk while boiling.
2. The milk will start to thicken as you are boiling it. Cook for 6-8 minutes and then remove from heat.
3. Allow the milk to cool to body temperature and follow Step 4 onwards to set this curd.

The chillies' method works because there is a substance in the caps that activates the bacteria required. However, it is not 100% reliable as temperature and humidity play a role. If you are trying for the first time, experiment with a very small quantity of thick milk first. Say, 1 cup and use 3-4 green chilli tops to set the curd.

YIELD – 1 LITRE CURD

USAGE
- Both the curds work well for *chhaach* and *raitas* or any recipe which is savoury and requires curd.
- Since plant-based curds do not sour like dairy yoghurt, you can use lemon or tamarind as a souring agent if required in a recipe. E.g. *kadhi* (see pg. 167)
- Soy curd will work for sweet recipes or curd drinks.
- Can be stored in the fridge for 5-6 days.

SAVOURY CASHEW CREAM

INGREDIENTS
1 cup cashews, soaked for 3-4 hrs, drained; Salt to taste

METHOD
1. Grind the cashews with a little salt and 1 tbsp water, or as needed, to move the blades.
2. Grind to a fine, smooth creamy paste.

YIELD – 1 CUP CREAM

USAGE
- Can be used to replace cream in any recipe, as a garnish to soups and curries, etc.
- Makes a great tasting dip, if you add some herbs and other seasonings, as desired.
- Use as a spread for sandwiches. High in calories, so great for growing kids who require more fat than adults.

SWEET CASHEW CREAM

INGREDIENTS
1 cup cashews, soaked for 3-4 hrs, drained ; 4-5 pitted dates or ½ cup sweet yellow raisins, soaked for 4 hours or more if the dates are hard

METHOD
1. Grind the cashews first, using as little of the dates' or raisins' soaking water, as required, to a smooth, creamy paste with no grittiness.
2. Add in the soaked dates or raisins and grind again using the sweet soaking water, as required.
3. Smoothen the cream as much as possible.

YIELD – 1 CUP CREAM

USAGE
- Can be used to replace sweet cream in any recipe.
- Can be stored in the fridge for up to 3-4 days.

If you use dates, they will give a darker colour to the cream than yellow raisins. The raisins might give a little sour taste so don't use in recipes where you don't need the sourness.

Sweet Cashew Cream

CASHEW MAYONNAISE

You will not believe how close this tastes to mayonnaise without using eggs, sugar, and oil, which are the regular high fat ingredients of conventional mayonnaise.

INGREDIENTS:
100 gm cashews, soaked for 3-4 hrs, drained; 1 tsp mustard seeds; 1 medium-sized onion, finely chopped; 2-3 cloves garlic; Water as required; Salt to taste

METHOD:
1. Grind the mustard seeds first. You can also use mustard sauce, if you wish.
2. Add the onion and garlic; grind to a fine paste.
3. Now add the cashews and salt to taste and grind again to a fine paste to a thick consistency like mayonnaise.

YIELD – ⅔ CUP

Cashew Mayonnaise

USAGE
• Use as a spread, dip or salad dressing.
• Can be stored in the fridge for up to a week.

CASHEW HERB CHEESE

INGREDIENTS
1 cup cashews, soaked for 3-4 hours, drained; Salt to taste; 1 clove garlic; ½ tsp dried mixed herbs; Black pepper powder, optional

METHOD
1. Grind the cashews, using as little water as required, to a smooth, creamy paste with no grittiness.
2. Pour in a large bowl to allow enough space for the cheese to ferment and rise up.
3. Cover loosely and let it sit for 8-12 hours. In hot and humid weather, it takes less time to ferment and in dry, cold weather it takes a longer time.
4. The way to know if your cheese is ready is to scrape the surface with a spoon and you should see large air bubbles made by the friendly bacteria. The cheese should also smell a little 'off'. When that happens, put it in the fridge to stop further fermentation.
5. To prepare the flavoured herb cheese, mix in the salt, crushed garlic clove and herbs and mix well.

YIELD –2 CUPS

Cashew Herb Cheese

USAGE
• Replace cheese in any savoury recipe e.g. pizza, lasagna, pasta, etc.
• Use as a sandwich spread or a dip.
• Can be stored in the fridge for up to 4 days.

ALMOND BUTTER

INGREDIENTS
2 cups raw almonds

METHOD
1. Roast the almonds, on low heat, till slightly brown.
2. Allow to cool slightly till warm.
3. In a dry grinder jar, put half the roasted almonds or just enough to cover the blades.
4. Grind till it turns from powder to butter. You may have to scrape the sides frequently or use the pulse function. Almonds take much longer

so be patient. If the machine heats up, give it rest

5. Almond butter may not yield oil in the home grinders as that requires professional or high powered grinders.

6. Remove the butter into a glass jar for storage and grind all the remaining almonds in this way.

YIELD – 1 CUP

USAGE

- Great in ice creams and also as butter replacements in cakes and cookies.
- Spread it on toast with a little date or maple syrup for a delightful snack.
- Stores outside the fridge for upto 2 months as long as you don't use a wet spoon.
- If you want raw almond butter, then no need to roast the almonds first and follow the same process. Store in the fridge for 1 month.

You can also make raw cashew butter with cashews using the same process as above.

Almond Butter

PEANUT BUTTER

INGREDIENTS

2 cups raw peanuts with skin; a pinch of rock salt

METHOD

1. Roast the peanuts on low heat till popping and brown. Stir them constantly to avoid burning. It can take approximately 20 minutes.
2. You know the peanuts are done when they are crunchy to eat upon cooling. Test a couple of peanuts to check. When done, allow to cool slightly till warm.
3. In a dry grinder jar, put half the still warm peanuts or just enough to cover the blades.
4. Grind with a pinch of salt till it turns from powder to butter. Use the pulse function if you need to stop and scrape too often. Finally, the butter may release a little oil, which is a good sign.
5. Remove the butter into a glass jar for storage and grind all the remaining peanuts in this way.

YIELD – 1 CUP BUTTER

USAGE

- Makes a great peanut sauce (see pg. 85)
- Replaces oil in baking.
- Have it straight on toast or a vegan cracker as an indulgence.
- Will stay outside the fridge for up to 2 months.

SESAME BUTTER (TAHINI)

INGREDIENTS

2 cups raw white sesame seeds

METHOD

1. Roast the sesame seeds on low heat till brown.
2. Allow to cool slightly till warm.
3. In a dry grinder jar, put half the roasted sesame or just enough to cover the blades.
4. Grind till it turns from powder to butter. It may release a little oil which is a good sign.
5. Remove the butter into a glass jar for storage and grind all the remaining seeds in this way.

YIELD – 1 CUP

USAGE

- Makes a great tahini dressing (see pg. 125)
- Replaces oil in baking.
- Used in Mediterranean spreads and dishes.
- Store outside the fridge for 2 months.

Sesame Butter (Tahini)

DATE OR RAISIN PASTE

INGREDIENTS
1 cup pitted dates or yellow raisins, washed and soaked for 6 hours or more if the dates are hard; 1 cup water for soaking

METHOD
1. In a wet grinder, grind the dates or raisins, with 1-2 tbsp soaking water, just enough to move the blades.
2. Add more water, if necessary, and keep grinding till you get a smooth paste.

YIELD - 1 CUP

USAGE
- Replaces sugar in all recipes.
- Date paste darkens the dish so works for chocolate or darker coloured recipes.
- Yellow raisins don't darken the dish as much. However, be careful in dessert recipes if they are sour as that may not be desirable. Check and buy only sweet raisins in this case or use dates instead.
- Can keep in the fridge for up to a week.

Some raisins are sour and cannot be used in a dessert unless the sourness is required. Sour raisins work very well in savoury sauces and curries. For desserts, it is better to use sweet raisins only. Yellow raisins will yield a lighter couloured paste, which will not darken your dish whereas dates or black raisins will darken the colour when added to a dish.

HOMEMADE TOMATO KETCHUP

INGREDIENTS
½ kg tomatoes, quartered; 1 small onion, quartered, optional; 3-4 cloves garlic, peeled, optional; ¼ cup raisins, soaked for 4 hours; 1 tsp ginger powder (*sonth*); ½ tsp rock salt; ¼ tsp garam masala; 1 tbsp any natural vinegar e.g. apple cider vinegar or rice vinegar

METHOD
1. Heat a pan with a tight fitting lid. Put the tomatoes, onion and garlic in a saucepan and cook, covered, on medium heat. Stir after 10 minutes when the tomatoes have released a lot of juice.
2. Continue to cook on medium heat till the tomatoes are quite soft. This should take another 5-7 minutes. Remove from heat allow to cool.
3. Blend to a paste and then put through a wire mesh strainer to remove the seeds and the skin.
4. Put the sauce in an open pan and boil for a few minutes to thicken the pulp.
5. In a wet grinder, blend the soaked raisins to make a smooth paste
6. Add the raisin paste to the boiling tomato pulp. Now add all the dry spices and cook another 2-3 minutes or till you have the desired consistency.
7. Remove from heat and set aside to cool. Add the vinegar and allow it to cool completely before bottling it. It will thicken further upon cooling.

YIELD - 300 ML

USAGE
- Replace store bought tomato ketchup, which has a lot of sugar and artificial chemicals.
- Will keep in the fridge for upto 5 days.

To get an even smoother sauce, you can smash and push the cooked tomatoes through the wire mesh, using the back of a big, round serving spoon. Then blend this paste with the cooked onions and garlic in a wet grinder. For a darker coloured sauce, you can use date paste instead of raisin paste.

TOMATO MILANESE SAUCE

INGREDIENTS
8 medium-sized tomatoes, chopped;
2 onions, finely chopped; 8 cloves garlic,
finely chopped; Salt and pepper to taste;
1 tsp dried / fresh oregano

METHOD
1. Dry-fry the onion and garlic in a pan
   until slightly brown.
2. Add in the tomatoes and allow them
   to cook for approximately 10 minutes
   till the consistency forms a paste.
3. Add salt and pepper to taste and
   oregano; mix well and use as required.

YIELD – 2 CUPS

USAGE
• Great in pasta, as a pizza spread and
  in lasagna, etc.
• Will keep in the fridge for up to 3 days.

FRESH VEGETABLE STOCK

INGREDIENTS
1 large onion, chopped; 1 large carrot,
chopped; 2 stalks of celery, chopped;
4 cloves garlic, chopped; 1 cup coriander
stems; 1 cup discarded stalks or leaves of
any vegetables e.g.: cauliflower, broccoli,
turnpis, etc. You can also use discarded
peels. 5 cups water; 2 tbsp fresh or
1 tbsp dried herbs like rosemary, thyme,
parsley, etc. 2 bay leaves; 5 whole black
peppercorns; Salt to taste

METHOD
1. Add some salt to the onion and allow
   it to 'sweat' for 10 minutes.
2. In a large pot, sauté the onion till brown.
   Add in the remaining vegetables and
   sauté for another 3-4 minutes.
3. Add the water and the remaining
   ingredients, tightly cover the pot and
   bring to the boil. Once it comes to the
   boil, lower heat and simmer for 20-25
   minutes till the vegetables are very
   soft but not disintegrated.
4. Use a large mesh strainer to sieve
   the stock. Mash the soft vegetables
   with the back of a ladle to get a
   thicker stock.

YIELD – 4-5 CUPS

USAGE
• Use as a base in soups.
• Use to replace oil to sauté vegetables
  or onions.
• Add instead of water in curries and
  sauces for additional flavour.
• Can keep in the fridge for 3 days or
  frozen for up to a month.

INDEX

INDIAN

AMERICAN

GRATITUDE

We would like to thank all the people who supported us without whom this book would not be in your hands.

Rachna Kapoor and Anil Narang for their good wishes, encouragement and generous support.

Lakhan and Malti, Mala's trusted team, who sweated out the summer with us with all the shopping, chopping, grinding, baking, grating, stirring, freezing, pouring and much much more.

Our friends, colleagues and clients who tested the recipes and gave us valuable feedback – Amber Lokhandwala, Ramesh Hirani, Hema Gopi, P.V. Narayanamoorthy, Devika Menon, Anita Chitkara, Dinakshi Arora, Millie Mitra, Preeta Pradhan and Bulbul Mankani.

Sneha Pamneja who did the layout and design and Priya Kapoor of Roli Books who took the challenge of publishing us as new authors in the area of vegan cooking, a nascent but growing trend in India.

Zorawar and Sikandar Shukla, Mala's two sons, for allowing us to pick their creative brains! Nandini's sister Shivani and niece Sara, who were supportive critics and participants in her many cooking experiments.

To all of you, we thank you from the bottom of our hearts in helping us make this dream a reality.

RESOURCES

IN YOUR QUEST TO KNOW MORE ABOUT THE VEGAN AND WHOLE-FOOD LIFESTYLE,
WE RECCOMMEND THAT YOU EXPLORE THE FOLLOWING BOOKS, VIDEOS, AND FILMS.

BOOKS:
World Peace Diet by Will Tuttle
Eat to Live by Dr. Joel Fuhrman, M.D.
The China Study by T. Colin Campbell
WHOLE by T. Colin Campbell
Reversing Diabetes by Dr. Neal Barnard , M.D.
There is a cure for diabetes by Dr. Gabriel Cousens, M.D.
Prevent and Reverse Heart Disease by Dr. Caldwell Esselstyn, M.D.
The Starch Solution by Dr. John McDougall, M.D.
Milk: A Silent Killer by Dr. NK Sharma
Healthy at 100 by John Robbins
You can also search for the video lectures by these authors on YouTube.

YOUTUBE VIDEOS:
Vegan Video Life Connected
PETA Glass Walls
The Last Heart Attack by CNN's Dr. Sanjay Gupta
Horrors in the Indian Dairy Industry

FILMS AND DOCUMENTARIES:
Earthlings (www.earthlings.com)
Forks over Knives (www.forksoverknives.com)
Cowspiracy – The Sustainability Secret (www.cowspiracy.com)
May I be Frank? (www.mayibefrankmovie.com)
Eating (www.eatingthemovie.com)
Vegucated (www.getvegucated.com)